Dreaming

is a universal phenomenon. Every individual dreams every night, even though he may not remember dreaming. Over the past twenty-five years Calvin S. Hall and Vernon J. Nordby have analyzed more than 50,000 dreams: from the dreams of an Ohio factory worker to a Swiss chemist to a woman psychologist; dreams reported by mountain climbers, by Australian aborigines, by school children, and by homosexuals; dream series published by Freud, Jung, Kafka, and Jack Kerouac.

THE INDIVIDUAL AND HIS DREAMS

In the introductory chapter, the authors explain that "our approach takes dreams as they are recalled and reported, analyzes them using standard procedures of content analysis, and tries to see how the resulting analysis enlarges our knowledge of the individual who has done the dreaming. Our aim is to take dreams out of the clinic and consulting room and to demonstrate their value for enlarging everyone's understanding of himself and of the world in which he lives."

CALVIN
NORDBY
of Califor
the author
chology a

D1593918

MENTOR Books of Related Interest

The Individual and His Dreams

*by Calvin S. Hall
and Vernon J. Nordby*

A SIGNET BOOK from
NEW AMERICAN LIBRARY
TIMES MIRROR

SIGNET TRADEMARK REG. U.S. PAT. OFF. AND FOREIGN COUNTRIES
REGISTERED TRADEMARK—MARCA REGISTRADA
HECHO EN CHICAGO, U.S.A.

SIGNET, SIGNET CLASSICS, SIGNETTE, MENTOR AND PLUME BOOKS
are published by The New American Library, Inc.,
1301 Avenue of the Americas, New York, New York 10019

FIRST PRINTING, MAY, 1972

PRINTED IN THE UNITED STATES OF AMERICA

To Bill Domhoff
Fellow Psychopomp

Contents

1. Introduction   9

2. Types of Dreams   19

3. Content Analysis   36

4. Symbols in Dreams   63

5. Consistencies in Dream Series   80

6. Dreams and Waking Behavior   103

7. Symbolism in Dreams and Waking Life   128

8. A Point of View   145

HOW TO ANALYZE YOUR OWN
DREAMS   156

Introduction   Collecting Dreams
Content Analysis
Inferences and Interpretations   Synthesis

Notes   193

References   199

Suggestions for Further Reading   203

Index   205

Chapter 1

Introduction °

During the past twenty-five years we have read and analyzed thousands of dreams. We are familiar with the dreams of Australian aborigines, Zulus, Nigerians, Navaho and Hopi Indians, Mexicans, Peruvians, Argentineans, American Negroes, and many other national and ethnic groups. We have analyzed dreams reported by climbers on the American Mount Everest expedition, dream diaries of a child molester and a blind man, and dreams of homosexuals, alcoholics, schizophrenics, transvestites, patients undergoing psychoanalysis, schoolchildren, college students, and people sleeping under laboratory conditions.

We have read dream series published by prominent people, those of Freud and Jung, Franz Kafka, Julian Green, William Dean Howells, Eugene Ionesco, Robert Lowie, Jack Kerouac, and Howard Nemerov. We have also read and analyzed dream diaries of more ordinary people: an Ohio factory worker, a British professor, a California secretary, a Santa Cruz surfer, a New England physiologist, a Pennsylvania schoolteacher, a Swiss chemist, a woman psychologist, a New York businessman, an Israeli official, a San Francisco writer, a Texas engineer, a Los Angeles high school student, and many others.

Our collection contains over fifty thousand dreams gathered from all over the world.

See Notes, p. 193 and References, p. 199, for further amplification of text and sources.

9

In 1953, eight years after we began our investigations, we published a book, *The Meaning of Dreams,* which discussed the results of our studies to that time. It was written for the general reader. Since 1953 we have made many other investigations using improved methods of analysis and we have written a number of articles and several books for professional audiences. (See page 193 for a complete list.) We feel it is once again time to survey for the general reader what we have learned about dreams.

The chief improvement we have made in analyzing dreams since 1953 consists of applying modern methods of content analysis to dreams. The older methods of analysis were subjective and qualitative, so that different analysts sometimes obtained conflicting results. The new methods, which will be discussed in Chapter 3, are objective and quantitative. When used by different investigators they yield comparatively the same results. The results obtained by content analysis can be treated mathematically, which is a big advantage in scientific research.

We will begin this book by presenting in the first chapter some of the conclusions we have reached, and then in subsequent chapters elaborate upon these conclusions by discussing the factual material upon which they are based. First, we would like to clarify our position on certain issues regarding dreams.

Our approach to dreams is fairly unusual. We are interested in the *contents,* or subject matter, of dreams and what they tell us about the dreamer and his behavior. Other investigators have been primarily interested in the *process* of dreaming—why we dream and the function or purpose of dreaming. Most of the well-known theories of dreaming concern themselves with causes and functions. It has been argued that dreaming is produced by an upset stomach, brain processes, external stimuli impinging upon a sleeping person, or the unconscious mind. The function of dreaming, it has been said, is to fulfill wishes, compensate for neglected aspects of the personality, resolve conflicts, reduce tension, return to a pleasurable past, or guard sleep. These are only a few of the theories that have been formulated during the past several thousand years.

The abundant literature on the causes and functions of dreaming is long on speculation and short on tested knowledge. The reason for this is that it is impossible to prove or disprove any of the theories. This is why theories of dreaming proliferate. Someone notices something new about dreams and proceeds to make a theory out of it. We suspect all modern theories have *some* truth in them, in the sense that they explain *some* dreams, but no theory explains all dreams. The ideal dream theory should be able to explain why a person had a specific dream at a specific time on a specific night.

Our approach takes dreams as they are recalled and reported, regardless of cause or purpose, analyzes them using standard procedures of content analysis, and tries to see how the resulting analysis enlarges our knowledge of the individual who has done the dreaming. Whatever their causes and functions may be, dreams may be used to good advantage. They have been employed advantageously in psychotherapy for over seventy years, not to mention their age-old use for prophesying the future. Our aim is to take dreams out of the clinic and consulting room and to demonstrate their value for enlarging everyone's understanding of himself and of the world in which he lives.

We started our investigations of dreams without any preconceptions of what we would find. We had no theory that we wished to prove or disprove. Gradually, we began to draw inferences from our findings. Whenever possible, we tried to test these inferences by making new investigations to see whether they were correct or not.

Throughout this book we have made an effort to distinguish between fact and inference. Unless one is vigilant, it is easy to treat opinion as fact and theory as truth without being aware of what one has done.

An example may help to clarify the distinction between fact and inference. It has been established by our investigations that dreams of misfortune outnumber dreams of good fortune. Many more bad things than good things happen to the dreamer in his dreams. We have never found an exception to this rule for individual dreams or groups of dreams, nor for female or male dream series. What this fact means is a matter of inference and interpretation. We infer from it that people conceive of the world as a predominantly threatening, unfriendly, hostile place. People everywhere, those who live in urban centers as well as those who live on the plains or in the jungles, adults as well as children, the privileged as well as the underprivileged, are basically insecure. This insecurity explains, we believe, why people erect defenses and make arrangements in their waking life to protect themselves from what they consider to be a hostile environment. It is more likely, as we shall try to show, that the hostile environment is a projection of their own hostile impulses. We will argue that man's insecurity stems more from his own nature than from his environment.

Other interpretations of the preponderance of threatening dreams are possible. One may believe that dreams go by opposites so that bad things in dreams are compensated for by good things in waking life. Or one may draw the inference from the high incidence of unpleasant dreams that people are basically masochistic; they really like to suffer. Or it may be that people feel guilty and so they punish themselves by having bad dreams. It has also been suggested we have just as many pleasant dreams as unpleasant ones but we tend to recall more of the unpleasant ones.

Many inferences can be drawn from the same fact. We must have the facts first, however, and that is what we have tried to provide in this book. The reader may choose to draw his own conclusions rather than to accept ours.

For those readers who are dissatisfied either with the facts as presented or our interpretations of them, we suggest they keep a record of their own dreams over a period of several months, preferably longer, and then analyze them using methods described in this book or those of their own devising. A person who does this will have an extremely rewarding experience in understanding dreams and understanding himself.

What precisely do we mean when we use the word "dream"? There are three possible meanings. It may refer to what one experiences while he is asleep. It may refer to what a person remembers when he awakens. Or it may denote what a person reports either verbally or in writing. That is, there is an *experienced* dream, a *remembered* dream, and a *reported* dream. It is only the reported dream that has any objective existence, since there is no way of telling what a person has dreamed or what he remembers until he describes it in words. Consequently, our studies can only deal with those dreams that are reported to us.

The necessity of having to depend upon reported dreams presents some difficulties. Some people cannot remember their dreams, or they remember so few that it is not worthwhile to analyze them. It has been our experience that when a person is properly motivated he can recall his dreams. If motivation fails, he can be brought into a sleep laboratory and awakened periodically throughout the night. Under these circumstances, he can recall as many as four or five dreams a night. It is possible that sleeping under laboratory conditions may affect his dreams. We investigated this question and found that dreams reported in the laboratory were different from those recalled under normal home conditions. Laboratory dreams tend to be more prosaic and less exciting than home dreams. There is less aggression and sex in laboratory dreams, and a greater preoccupation with the dreamer's normal waking activities.

The fact that some people cannot remember their dreams is not a serious impediment to research. There are enough people who can remember their dreams to supply us with all we need for our studies.

People differ in their ability to describe a dream. Children do not have the verbal ability of adults. Consequently, their dream reports are apt to be much shorter than those of older people. People with more education usually give fuller descriptions than people with less education. Differences in length of report are not too significant, however, because a short report ordinarily contains the essential features of a dream. What children and less educated people leave out are details that are of minor importance.

The handicap of differences in verbal ability can be overcome to some extent by acquainting a person beforehand with the points he should try to cover in his report. We make it a practice of asking a person to include the following information, if possible:

1. the *setting* or locale in which the dream took place,
2. the *characters* who appeared in the dream, their sex and age, and whether known persons or strangers,
3. the *actions* and *interactions* in which the dreamer and the other persons engaged,
4. the *objects* he saw, and
5. the *emotions* or feelings he felt during the dream.

With a little practice, virtually any person can learn to describe a dream.

Extensive questioning of the dreamer after he has reported a dream should be avoided since it may lead him to tell things that did not actually appear in the dream, in order to please the questioner or because it has been suggested to him.

Two other obstacles to obtaining accurate dream reports are conscious suppression and intentional deception. Some remembered dreams are not told because the person is ashamed of them or because they touch upon matters related to the dreamer's emotional stability, his feelings about people close to him, or other private affairs he would rather not divulge to an outsider. Sex dreams, particularly those that involve aberrant practices, may not be told.

A person may make up a dream. Made-up dreams are fairly easy to recognize. They are either simple wishful fantasies or they are absurd or they are devoid of visual imagery. Harder to spot is the authentic dream in which some important detail has been altered or omitted. A young man may dream he was having sex with another man and report he was making love with a woman. Or a woman who dreams of having sexual relations with a strange man may report she was having sex with her husband.

Fortunately, these impediments are less common than one might think. It has been our experience that people in general are truthful in reporting what they dreamed. The dreamers remain anonymous through the use of code names, and no personal relationship exists between the dreamer and the investigator while the dreams are being collected. Moreover, there is no lack of dreams in our collection in which the most distasteful and shameful things happen. Fathers and mothers are murdered by the dreamer. The dreamer has sex with members of his family. He rapes, pillages, tortures, and destroys. He performs all kinds of obscenities and perversions. He often does these things without remorse, and even with considerable glee.

One reason for this candor is that people do not feel responsible for what they dream. A dream is something that happens while they are asleep and they feel they do not have control over it as they do over events in waking life.

In a number of respects, dreams are a unique form of experience. They occur during sleep when a person is relatively insulated and isolated from the external world. He is free, relatively speaking, to dream without the usual inhibitions, obligations, and persecutions imposed by the external world.

Dreams are often intensely visual in character in contrast to the more imageless thoughts of waking life. They are more like perceptions than thoughts. Dreams appear unannounced and without any intention, volition, or effort on the part of the dreamer. They are happenings over which the dreamer has no control, unlike thinking and imagining during waking life. They seem to create themselves and to unwind like a motion picture or play in which the dreamer is both audience and actor.

Although dreams are imaginary, the dreamer does not

distinguish them from reality as a person does with his waking fantasies and daydreams. While he is dreaming, everything seems real and plausible. A dreamer can die or he can be reborn. He can be a child again. He can fall from a cliff without hurting himself, fly or float through the air, and perform other feats that would be impossible to perform in waking life. People he has not seen or thought of for years enter his dreams, and people long dead are alive again. He travels in countries he has never visited and associates with famous people he has never met. Scenes can change instantaneously, and days, months, and even years are compressed into seconds.

The dream is so natural to the dreamer that his feelings are usually those he would experience were he awake and in the situation. He is alarmed when he teeters on the edge of a cliff, panic-stricken when he is chased by a wild animal, exultant when he flies through the air, frustrated when he encounters an insurmountable obstacle, embarrassed when he appears naked in public, overjoyed when he finds a lot of money and heartbroken when he loses it, angry when his girlfriend jilts him, guilty when he is apprehended doing something wrong, proud when he succeeds and downcast when he fails. There is evidence to suggest that people with weak hearts may be frightened to death by a traumatic dream.

The plausibility of dreams while they are being dreamed, even when they are totally unrealistic and irrational, suggests that they may be expressions of a deeper and more profound reality than we are aware of in waking life. Dreams may have their own truth and their own logic, which is different from the reality and logic of mundane existence. They may exist in a domain which lies on the other side of the looking glass of everyday life. Nonetheless, their relevance for understanding mundane existence is very important.

In view of the apparent reality of dreams, it is not surprising that many people used to believe dreams were actual and not imaginary experiences. The soul was thought to leave the body during sleep, and what we call dreams were regarded as being the actual experiences of this disembodied soul. This theory is still believed by some people today.

Dreams vary in length and complexity. Some dreams consist of a single scene in which nothing much happens. Other dreams are very complex, consisting of several scenes and implicating a variety of characters, objects, and actions. A dream may have a well-organized plot, like a short story. Often a dream appears to have no well-defined beginning or ending. It is experienced as an excerpt from a longer dream, as though one had gone to a play after it had started and left before the final curtain.

Some dreams are so vivid they can be remembered for years without fading; others are so hazy the dreamer has difficulty recalling them.

Dreaming is a universal phenomenon. No group of people has ever been found who are ignorant of what it means to dream. Historical records provide ample evidence that people have always dreamed and have always been interested in their dreams. In some societies, dreams play a decisive role in determining how individuals will conduct themselves and what their status will be. Important decisions are often determined by dreams.

Whether animals other than man dream is a matter for speculation, since they are unable to report their dreams. Most people believe they do because they have seen their pet dog or cat move in apparently purposeful ways during sleep. There is no reason why animals should not dream, and some scientific investigations suggest that they do.

Not only is dreaming universal but *every* individual dreams *every* night and throughout the night. This can be demonstrated by awakening people at random and asking them if they have been dreaming. Dreams have been reported from such awakenings at any time during the night. Dreaming may be a continuous process during sleep.

The subject matter of dreams is inexhaustible. One can dream about anything, from the most commonplace to the most bizarre and outrageous happening. The world of dreams appears to be a world without limits.

Despite the diversity of subject matter of dreams, a number of common themes have been found in all of the sets and series of dreams we have studied. A *set* of dreams consists of a number of dreams obtained from a group of people who share some characteristic in common, for example, they are the same age, sex, or nationality. A *series* of dreams is a number of dreams reported by the same person. We have already noted that dreams of misfortune are universal. So are dreams of being chased and attacked, of sex and aggression, of success and failure, of frustration and gratification, of food and eating, of animals and supernatural beings, of family members, friends, and strangers, of individuals and groups, of falling and flying, and many other things.

There are many variations on a particular theme. One may

dream of being chased by a man or a group of men, by an animal or a monster, by a supernatural being, or by an object. The person doing the chasing may carry a gun, a knife, a spear, a club, or a whip. We call these variations that have essentially the same significance *conceptual equivalents*.

Some themes are more characteristic of the dreams of one sex than the other, of one age group than another, and of a particular nationality or ethnic group. (We intend to discuss sex, age, and ethnic differences in dream contents in another volume.)

Although all of the universal themes will be found in a long series of dreams, the frequency with which the themes occur varies from dreamer to dreamer. Each dream series has its own individual characteristics.

When one analyzes a dream diary that has been kept over a number of years, a large amount of consistency in what the person dreams about is found from year to year. He is dreaming about many of the same themes at the age of fifty as he was at the age of twenty-five. This consistency occurs in spite of fairly drastic changes in the conditions of his waking life. Such consistency suggests to us that dreams have a timeless quality; that is, they are not substantially altered by the passage of time.

Where do the contents of dreams come from? They come from a number of sources: from the lifetime experiences of the dreamer, from conditions in the dreamer's immediate sleep environment, and from his physiological state during sleep. Memories of childhood experiences as well as those of the present contribute to the subject matter of dreams. It is possible that memories laid down during prenatal life provide material for dreams. Some authorities believe inherited predispositions contribute to the contents of dreams. Any particular dream may contain material from all of these sources.

Why one should have just this dream at this particular time of the night is a question that cannot be answered. Nor does it need to be. Given a long enough series of dreams, we can be fairly sure that the person's dream life has been adequately sampled. It is not even necessary to know the sources of dreams in order to use them for self-understanding. The fact that a person dreams about a childhood experience thirty years afterwards indicates that the experience is still very much alive in his memory.

One of the oldest and most persistent ideas about dreams is that some of the elements of a dream may be symbolic. They mean something other than what they appear to mean. A spider is not a spider but a symbol for the dreamer's mother. A gun is not a gun but a symbol for the penis. Going into a cave represents a return to the womb and coming out of the water represents being born. One difficulty with this idea is that it is virtually impossible to tell when a dream element is to be regarded as symbolic and when it is to be accepted for what it is. One can ignore the whole question of symbolism and still learn a great deal about a person from his dreams. Or one can make inferences as to the symbolic meaning of an element and see whether these inferences help to enlarge one's understanding of the dreamer. We shall discuss methods of decipering symbols in Chapter 4.

We have learned a great deal about symbolism in everyday life from studying symbolism in dreams. Even the most commonplace objects and activities are loaded with symbolic significance when seen through the eyes of the dreamer. The study of dreams enriches our appreciation of the everyday world.

We are chiefly interested in dreams because of what they can tell us about waking behavior and personality. Our studies clearly indicate that there is a close correspondence between what a person dreams about and what he does and thinks when he is awake. He remains pretty much the same person awake or asleep. We call this the *continuity principle*.

Not only do we learn a great deal about the individual from analyzing his dreams but we can also learn a great deal about the nature of society and its institutions by studying large sets of dreams.

These, then, are some of the topics that will be discussed in this book. After twenty-five years of working with dreams, we are more firmly convinced than ever that dreams are much too important to be neglected or ignored. Dreams furnish us with indispensable information about human nature and human society. We hope the evidence presented in this book will convince the reader of the truth of this statement.

Chapter 2

Types of Dreams

After reading several hundred dream reports, one begins to notice that some themes keep repeating themselves over and over again. By saying the same theme, we mean the same basic plot or event. This is true for individual dream series as well as for sets of dreams obtained from groups of people. These *typical dreams*, as we shall call them, are experienced by virtually every dreamer, although there are differences in the frequency with which these themes occur among individual dreamers and among groups of dreamers. The same general theme may also appear in many variations.

One of the most prevalent types is the dream in which an aggression occurs. In a sample of one thousand dreams obtained from young adult male and female Americans, nearly half of the dreams contained at least one aggression, and in many of them there were two, three, four, and even five aggressions. This high incidence of aggression is true not only for Americans but also for many other nationality and ethnic groups whose dreams we have studied. For example, 70 percent of the dreams collected from Zulus contained at least one aggression. The comparable figures for some other ethnic groups are: Yir Yoront living in Australia, 65 percent; Alorese, 60 percent; Uganda and Hopi each 55 percent. At the other end of the scale are the Navajo and Mexicans, with 33 percent of their dreams containing an aggression. Children's dreams contain almost twice as much aggression as adult dreams do. Much of the child's aggression is with animals.

The intensity of the aggression runs the gamut from unexpressed feelings of hostility to murder. Some idea of the high incidence of murder in dreams can be gained from the following figures. The total number of human characters in one thousand dreams reported by young Americans was approximately 3,500. This figure includes the dreamers as well as all other characters mentioned in their dream reports. Of these 3,500 characters, 23 were murdered, which yields a rate of nearly one murder for every 150 characters. The annual current rate of murders committed in the United States is about one out of every 14,000 persons.

Aggression takes the form of quarreling, disobedience, coercion, exploitation, accusation, threat, chasing, arresting, confining, destruction, rape, and physical assault. Some aggressive dreams are very brutal.

Franz Kafka, the famous writer, who was a peace-loving person in his waking life, had the following dream.

Two groups of men were fighting each other. The group to which I belonged had captured one of our opponents, a gigantic naked man. Five of us clung to him, one by the head, two on either side by his arms and legs. Unfortunately we had no knife with which to stab him. But since for some reason there was no time to lose, and an oven stood nearby whose extraordinary huge cast-iron door was red-hot, we dragged the man to it, held one of his feet close to the oven until the foot began to smoke, pulled it back again until it stopped smoking, then thrust it close to the door again.

One of our dream correspondents, a middle-aged professional man who has not had a physical fight since he was a boy, reported the following dream.

I am engaged in a gun battle with people I know. I shoot them down one at a time. An associate at the place I work is grinning. I don't wait to see whether he is armed. I smilingly put a .45 slug through his gut. I continue to kill people one by one.

He reported feeling "intense pleasure at destruction, joy in killing, tremendous satisfaction, having a ball."

Women also have sadistic dreams. Here is an example reported by a young woman.

I was living with a young man. My father was in our way, so we killed him. Or rather, my companion did the killing by lashing the victim with a whip while I looked on. He wrapped the corpse in a white sheet and laid it on a step. There it lay for all the world to see, and I remember blood upon the dead face.

Children's dreams can also be bloodthirsty, as illustrated by this dream reported by a seven-year-old boy.

I was in a place where there were lots of castles. A king came over to me and said, "If you don't shoot that man over there with an arrow, you'll get your head chopped off." I took my bow and arrow and shot the man through the neck. The man screamed. The king said, "Okay, now I'll arrest you for murder." Then two men chopped me in two with big swords.

Aggressive dreams can be classified in various ways. The dreamer may be either one of the participants in the aggression or he may witness other characters in the dream quarreling or fighting. Most of the time he is actively involved either as the one who initiates the aggression or as the victim of aggression by another character. More often he is the victim. In all of the groups whose dreams we have analyzed, the dreamer sees himself as the victim about two-thirds of the time, on the average. Navajo dreamers are victims 89 percent of the time whereas their neighbors, the Hopi, are victims only 60 percent of the time. There are, of course, differences among individual dreamers, and in some dream series the dreamer is more often the aggressor than the victim. Children especially see themselves in their dreams as victims of attack either by adults or by animals. Women dream slightly more often of being victims than men do.

A further breakdown of aggressive dreams consists of identifying the character or characters in each dream with whom the dreamer had an aggression. This analysis can be as detailed as one wishes to make it. One may classify the characters with whom the dreamer is having aggressive encounters into humans and animals, males and females, and those who are familiar or unfamiliar to the dreamer.

When an animal appears in a dream it usually plays the role of an aggressor. This is a frequent type of dream in childhood but it is also common among adult dreamers. The animal may be either wild or domesticated, and the type of animal includes virtually all species. Children have been chased or attacked in their dreams by dogs, cats, horses, lions, bears, gorillas, snakes, alligators, tigers, wolves, elephants, bulls, dragons, boars, turtles, and spiders.

Dreamers, be they children or adults, males or females, Americans or Zulus, have more aggressive encounters with male characters than with female characters. Male dreamers engage in more aggression with strangers than with people known to them. Female dreamers have an equal number of aggressions with familiar and unfamiliar persons. Next to animals, the *male stranger* is the most frequent enemy of the dreamer and the one with whom the dreamer has the most serious aggressions.

At least two theories have been advanced to explain why animals and male strangers are the chief enemies of dreamers. Freudian theory states that animals and male strangers are disguised representations of the dreamer's father. The child's first enemy is his father. He is the original stranger whom the son or daughter fears. This fear can exhibit itself in diminished or increased forms through life, depending on the first crucial years of the child-father relationship. There is a good deal of evidence which supports this theory.

The following study was made of a group of dreams which had been free-associated to by the dreamers. We selected from the free associations those which had been made to male strangers appearing in the dreams. In their associations, the dreamers frequently mentioned their own father or someone else's father or a father-like person such as a male teacher, minister, or army officer.

In another study we used the animal-as-father hypothesis to great advantage in solving one of the most perplexing problems we faced in analyzing a dream series. The person who recorded his dreams had been arrrested, found guilty, and imprisoned a number of times for molesting children. He gave his diary of nearly 1400 dreams to us to analyze, hoping that the analysis would shed some light on the reasons for his abnormal behavior.

The method of analysis we use (which will be described in greater detail in the next chapter) starts by counting the number of times each class of characters appears in a series of dreams. A class may consist of a specific person such as the dreamer's mother, father, brother, best friend, or employer, or it may be a larger group of persons such as males, females, children, policemen, or prominent persons.

The child molester dreamed frequently about his mother and sister with whom he lived when he was not confined to an institution. Not once in all the 1400 dreams did he dream about his father. The absence of the father suggested two possible hypotheses. Either the father had died or left the family while the dreamer was still a baby, or the father had done something to his son which caused the son to banish him from his dreams.

If the second hypothesis were correct, it might be expected that the father would appear in a disguised form in his son's dreams. On the assumption that one such disguise would be an animal form, we looked through the dreams for the presence of animals. One animal dream, in particular, caught our attention. This is the dream.

A bull that seemed to have human intelligence came behind me and held me against him. I did not like his advances and I sensed that he wanted to have sexual relations with me. So I broke away from him.

We inferred from this dream that the bull stood for the father and that the attack stood for a sexual assault on the boy by his father. Here, then, was a possible reason why the father had been repressed from the son's dreams. More importantly, the dream suggested that the dreamer really had been sexually assaulted in childhood by his father. Then when the son grew up, he molested children just as his father had molested him.

These inferences proved to be correct. Beginning when the child was four years old and for several years thereafter, he had been repeatedly forced to perform fellatio (oral intercourse) on his father. The boy enjoyed it, although afterwards he had severe guilt feelings and conflicts over doing it. The guilt feelings may have caused him to repress dreaming about his father, but they did not prevent him from copying his father in waking life.

This example illustrates the value that a particular theory may have for pointing the way to a solution of a problem. Theories provide us with useful guidelines, although sometimes they may lead us astray. We have found the theories propounded by Freud and Jung especially useful because they used dream analysis so extensively in treating their patients.

A second theory that offers an explanation why animals and male strangers are often our enemies in dreams is identified with the Jungian school of psychoanalysis. For Jung, animals and male strangers stand for aspects of the dreamer's own personality. Animals represent the primitive, animalistic side of man's nature. Jung called this the *shadow*. (Jung's shadow is similar to Freud's *id*. Freud believed animals in dreams could also represent the *id*.) Jung believed that what is neglected or repressed in waking life is compensated for in dreams. Since man tends to repress the animal side of his nature by day, he dreams about animals by night.

It is true that the child molester did attempt to suppress his wayward sexual impulses, but unfortunately for him and for his victims he was not always successful in waking life, and much less so in his dream life.

Male strangers, according to Jungian theory, represent the masculine aspect of personality from which the individual has become estranged. The child molester had rejected his masculinity because he considered it to be dangerous. In fact, he sought psychological help when he recognized that the affectionate behavior toward children which he customarily displayed was becoming more aggressively sexual.

Although aggression is very common in dreams, there are large differences among people in the amount of aggression that occurs in their dreams. We have analyzed dream series in which the frequency of aggression with dream characters runs as high as 65 percent and as low as 5 percent. These differences among dreamers raises an interesting question. Does the person who has a lot of aggression in his dreams also experience a lot of aggression in waking life? And does the person who has little aggression in his dreams experience little aggression in waking life? We will discuss the relationship between dreams and waking behavior in Chapter 6.

Intentional acts of self-aggression are rare in dreams. Suicide virtually never occurs. Self-punishment is quite common, though. It takes two principal forms. One is the dream in which the dreamer is the victim of attack by another character or group of characters. The dreamer is having himself punished because he feels guilty for something he has done or thought. It is a well-known fact of human psychology that children as well as adults often do something to invite punishment. Punishment assuages their feelings of guilt. People have been known to commit criminal acts in waking life out of a sense of guilt. They want to be convicted and punished.

The other form that self-punishment takes is misfortune. Dreams of misfortune are typical, occurring in one out of every three dreams. Anything harmful that happens to the dreamer or to another character which is not the result of an aggressive interaction is classified as a misfortune. If a person breaks his arm in a fight, that is classed as an aggression. If he breaks his arm as a result of an accident, that is a misfortune.

Various types of misfortune occur in dreams: death, bodily injury or illness, destruction of, injury to, or loss of a possession, threats from the environment, falling, and frustration. Included under frustration are such experiences as encountering an obstacle, inability to move, being lost, missing an airplane, train, or boat, being late for work or an appointment, and finding oneself in an embarrassing situation such as appearing nude in public. There are more deaths in dreams resulting from misfortune than deaths resulting from aggression: 38 accidental deaths versus 31 murders occurred in a thousand dreams.

One may break down dreams of injury to the body into the specific parts of the body that are affected. A dreamer may hurt his hand, break a leg, bump his head, have a heart attack, lose his hair, injure an eye, or have a tooth fall out. Dreams of bodily disorders have been used to diagnose an incipient physical condition that has not developed to the point where there are observable symptoms. If a person dreams of being short of breath, this dream may presage the beginning of a respiratory disorder.

Injury to a part of the body may signify that the dreamer holds that body part responsible for his misconduct. The voyeur may dream about losing his eyesight. "If the eye offends, pluck it out."

According to Freudian theory, injury to certain parts of the body represent castration anxiety. A person punishes himself for indulging in sexual fantasies by dreaming about cutting a finger, losing a tooth or his hair, or breaking a limb. Castration in dreams may also be represented by an injury to or loss of something belonging to the dreamer, such as having a flat tire or crumpled fender, losing a pen or pencil, or trying to shoot a defective gun.

We used this theory to test the hypothesis that males have more castration anxiety than females do. Women are supposed to have less castration anxiety because they feel (unconsciously) they have already been castrated. In our study, we found that bodily disabilities and injuries or defects to something belonging to the dreamer were three times more numerous in male dreams than in female dreams.

Probably every person, sooner or later, will dream about hair or teeth. We examined a large number of dreams in which hair or teeth were mentioned, and discovered that the prevailing theme of these dreams was *loss*. Teeth crumbled, fell out, or were extracted, and hair fell out or was cut. Here are two vivid dental dreams reported by young women.

> I dreamed that my front teeth were loose and wobbled. Then I thought I was chewing something hard. I spit what I was chewing into my hand and looked at it. My hand was full of blood and teeth. My mouth felt sore and swollen.

> I was talking with a group of people. Suddenly I heard a crunching noise and felt something drop into my mouth. I spit it into my hand and saw it was a tooth. It seemed to be an eye tooth but resembled a three-legged individual salt dish. I remarked upon the oddity to my friends only to feel a sudden avalanche of falling teeth.

This is a hair dream reported by a young man.

> I was standing in front of a mirror combing my hair. Tremendous amounts came out, and when I was through I was practically bald. It didn't bother me much at first, and then I suddenly realized that this hair I had lost was lost for life, and there was nothing I could do to get it back.

A secondary theme found in dental dreams is that of being chased by an animal with large, sharp teeth. This theme is illustrated by the following dream reported by a young man.

> I dreamed that I was in a large open space and huge animals of all sorts with wide open mouths and big gnashing teeth were chasing me. I ran from side to side trying to escape. The huge animal monsters finally hemmed me in. They were going to claw and eat me. I awoke.

The theme of loss of hair and teeth in dreams is not surprising since these parts of the body *are* cut or fall out. Children are often alarmed by having their hair cut or by losing their teeth. Nor does it take a very large inferential leap to see an association between loss of hair or teeth, or being chased by an animal with large teeth, and threat to or loss of the genitals.

The two ways by which a dreamer can punish himself, either by being the victim of attack or by suffering a misfortune, are different psychologically. As a victim, one can absolve himself of blame for the attack. He is, after all, a helpless and guiltless victim. It is less easy to blame a misfortune on another person. The dreamer himself must bear the brunt of the blame. It is interesting that females dream more often of being victims of aggression, and males more often of being victims of misfortune. This difference may be explained by the Freudian theory that the conscience of the woman differs from the conscience of the man. Her conscience is said to be more externalized. This means she is less likely to accept responsibility for her misdeeds. The male conscience is more internalized, which means he is more likely to acknowledge his own guilt and to blame himself for his misdeeds.

Contrasted with the high incidence of misfortune dreams is the very low frequency of dreams in which a good fortune occurs. This difference, as we have mentioned before, holds true for every set and series of dreams we have analyzed.

Another universal finding is that the misfortune happens more often to the dreamer than it does to other characters in his dreams. When the misfortune happens to the dreamer, it represents, as we have said, self-punishment; when it happens to another character it is a thinly disguised expression of the hostility the dreamer feels toward that character. If a person dreams of the death of someone close to him, that may be the expression of a death wish. One dreamer, for example, dreamed that his father died of a heart attack, following which the dreamer himself experienced a heart attack. In this case, the death wish toward the father was swiftly followed by retribution. If a person dreams a friend has an auto accident, that may express a hostile wish against the friend. Some dreamers have few aggression dreams but compensate for the lack of outright hostility by having many misfortunes happen to other people.

There is a special type of misfortune dream in which a person relives an actual unpleasant experience he has been through. It was first observed in shell-shocked soldiers who dreamed recurrently about a terrifying battle experience. According to Freud, this traumatic dream represents an attempt to master the overwhelming flood of anxiety caused by the original experience.

In a dream series of an older woman, she dreamed repeatedly of the circumstances of her husband's death. This could not be called a death wish dream because he had already died. His death occurred suddenly early one morning in their bedroom. Freud would say she recreated the situation in her dreams in an attempt to subdue the original shock. She also dreamed of his being alive again, which is an obvious wish-fulfillment dream. These wish-fulfillment dreams were much less common than dreams of his death or of losing him. Out of 48 dreams in which her husband appeared, 39 made reference to his illness and dying or to the dreamer losing him, and only 9 had him appearing alive and well or returning. As the years went by after his death, the number of wish-fulfillment dreams decreased to the vanishing point, whereas dreams of death and separation increased.

Sex and aggression, according to some theories of personality, are two of the basic motivating forces in human life and society. Although this may be disputed for waking behavior, it is certainly true for dream behavior. Overt sexual dreams, although they are usually less frequent than aggressive dreams and dreams of misfortune, are still fairly common. It is believed that many dreams which are not openly sexual in character contain disguised or symbolic references to sexual activity. We will not consider symbolized erotic dreams at this time but devote our attention to clearly defined sexual dreams.

Two of the most interesting features of sex dreams are the great variety of sexual activity that takes place and the diversity of partners with whom the dreamer has sexual interactions. A male dreamer may have sex with females, males, and animals. They may be the dreamer's spouse or girlfriend, close relatives, acquaintances, or strangers. They may even be physical objects. One dreamer had sexual intercourse with a knothole, one experienced orgasm while climbing a tree, a third ejaculated while he was walking along a railroad track, and another reached a climax while mowing the grass. Outright masturbation rarely occurs in dreams, but oral stimulation by the dreamer of his own penis does occur. Few men are able to perform this acrobatic feat in waking life.

The kinds of sexual activities in which dreamers engage include all possible variations: coitus, anal intercourse or sodomy, fellatio, cunnilingus, analingus, and others. There are also all kinds of foreplay activities: kissing, embracing, caressing the breasts and other erogenous parts of the body, and so forth.

The diversity of sexual acts and partners is illustrated by the following examples. The first individual for whom we have a large number of sex dreams is a thirty-year-old male. He is a college teacher who is interested in dreams. His dream diary contained 276 dreams of which 69 were overt sex dreams in which he was actively participating. He also witnessed others having sex, but we will not be concerned with these voyeuristic dreams. His sexual partners and the number of times he had sexual relations with each of them in these 69 dreams were as follows.

wife	19 times
mother	12 times
daughter	once
aunt	once
women friends	9 times
female strangers	5 times
nurse	twice
prostitute	twice
father	twice
brother	twice
men friends	8 times
male strangers	once
masturbation	once
self-fellatio	once
swimming	once
knothole	once

With these partners, he engaged in conventional intercourse, anal intercourse, fellatio, cunnilingus, analingus, and masturbation. Some sexual acts were performed while other people were watching. Some of the sexual dreams were satisfying while others were dissatisfying or disgusting. His most pleasurable sex dream was one in which his wife was asleep (in the dream) while he copulated with her. His conception of sex as revealed in his dreams was primarily aggressive, exploitative, and even sadistic. Rarely did he show any tenderness, affection, or consideration for his partner. Here are several examples.

I am having anal intercourse with my father and stabbing him in the back with a knife.

My mother comes into my room. When she comes near my bed, I grab her, pull her into bed, and rape her.

I am performing cunnilingus on a girl while she is performing fellatio on me.

I am having anal intercourse with a man. The thrusts of my penis is a torture that he can hardly bear.

In waking life, this dreamer's outlets have been limited to his wife, rare encounters with other women, and masturbation, which he did not begin until he was twenty years old.

He has never had sex with his mother, daughter, aunt, father, brother or any other male, except one time when he was a boy. He is very much preoccupied with sex in his waking life as well as in his dreams.

Our second dreamer is a married man with one daughter. He is also a college teacher. His dream diary contained 839 dreams, of which 200 were sex dreams. His sexual partners were many and varied. Dozens of different male and female friends and acquaintances appeared in these sex dreams, and they ranged in age from six to eighty.

wife	3 times
daughter	5 times
women friends	21 times
female strangers	17 times
little girl	once
prominent female	once
brothers	3 times
male relative	once
men friends	93 times
male strangers	46 times
prominent males	5 times
little boy	twice
self-fellatio	once
masturbation	once

Like the previous dreamer, this man also engaged in a variety of sexual acts, but unlike the other dreamer, a great deal of affection and tenderness was displayed. Kissing and embracing were common, while exploitation and aggression were almost nonexistent.

It will be noted that this dreamer had predominantly homosexual dreams (150 out of 200 sex dreams), although in waking life his sexual contacts were primarily with women during most of the time that the dream diary was kept. More recently he has become exclusively homosexual. According to him, his sex life is more satisfying since the change took place, which suggests that the dreams told the dreamer something important about his latent impulses.

The third example is an unmarried man in his forties who lives with his mother and sister. He has been convicted several times for molesting children. This person had 158 sex dreams out of a total of 1368 dreams. He had contacts with the following classes of characters.

sister	12 times
adult female strangers	59 times
adolescent females	9 times
female children	29 times

known adult males	9 times
adult male strangers	16 times
male adolescents	8 times
male children	10 times
babies and children	4 times
animals	twice

This person's sex dreams differ from those of the two previous individuals in the large number of sexual contacts with children and adolescents. Many of his dreams consist of sexual thoughts and fantasies without any actual body contact. This is true in his waking behavior as well. He has had very few sexual relationships, and never with an adult female, although he tried once without success.

It will be noted that the child molester had fewer sex dreams, one out of ten, as compared with one out of four for each of the two previous dreamers. They both had a more active sex life in reality than the child molester did.

The number of different sex partners that a person can have is illustrated by the dreams of a married man in his thirties. Over a three-year period he recorded 64 dreams in which he had sexual intercourse with 40 different individuals. They were:

> his wife
> 18 known women
> Sophia Loren
> a prostitute
> a Negro woman
> a Spanish woman
> an Arabian woman
> a witch
> 13 female strangers
> his brother
> a male angel

In addition, he masturbated to orgasm once and engaged in auto-fellatio twice in dreams. Aside from masturbation, which he engaged in frequently, this man's sexual outlets in waking life were limited to his wife, with whom he had coitus infrequently, and when he did it was with little gratification.

Dreamers differ in the number of sex dreams they have. One of our dreamers, a healthy young married man, had very few sex dreams, and those few were almost always with his wife. In waking life, he also infrequently engaged in sexual relations, even with his wife. As we shall see in a later chapter, his sexual energy seems to have been dissipated in a variety of strenuous physical activities.

We would not like to leave the reader with the impression that dreams are exclusively concerned with aggression, misfortune, and sex. They are not. There are, for example, a number of simple wish-fulfillment dreams. Children dream of receiving presents, adolescent boys of performing outstanding feats in the playground or battlefield, college students of passing examinations, young men of becoming famous, young women of wearing beautiful clothes and jewels, older women of living in spacious mansions, and almost everyone of finding large sums of money. But such dreams are in the minority. We examined 100 dreams reported by children between the ages of two and twelve, when simple wish-fulfillment dreams are supposed to be most common, and found only 12 that could be classified as wish fulfillments.

There are also a number of dreams in which the dreamer is having a good time at a party, playing a game, going on an outing, or talking with friends. Many times, however, the good time is interrupted by something unpleasant. The dreamer gets sick and has to leave the party, he hurts himself while playing a game, a thunderstorm spoils the outing, or something interrupts the conversation. Many wedding dreams are marred because the dreamer appears inappropriately dressed, is marrying an unsuitable partner, is prevented from getting to the church, or trips while walking down the aisle. It would appear that man cannot enjoy himself in his dreams for very long without paying a price for his pleasure.

People also do kind and helpful things for other people in their dreams. In 50 consecutive dreams recorded by a middle-aged woman, she did the following friendly acts:

> Took care of an abandoned baby
> Expressed gratitude to a man
> Carried a can of paint for a woman friend
> Did a favor for a woman friend
> Prevented a woman friend from falling
> Served coffee to a male friend
> Bought lunch for a little girl
> Took care of baby mice

In the *same* 50 dreams that she was performing these eight friendly acts, she was being aggressive toward people and animals 28 times and suffering a misfortune 23 times.

There are two other kinds of dreams that are quite typical. These are dreams in which reference is made to food and eating, and going to the bathroom. Both of these types of dreams refer to essential bodily needs, but many of them have psychological overtones. For example, instead of simply relieving oneself in the bathroom, the dream is often complicated by the dreamer not being able to locate a bathroom, by finding someone already in the bathroom, or by being interrupted by someone coming in. He frequently chooses an inappropriate place to urinate or defecate, and sometimes he is embarrassed by having others stare at him.

Eating dreams are rarely simple either. The food is spoiled, burned, or tastes bad. The dreamer sits in a restaurant waiting in vain to be served, or the food is removed before he has a chance to taste it. Sometimes the dreamer gets sick while he is eating.

There are other typical dreams: getting married and having children (especially by women), buying something, receiving a letter, taking an examination, making a telephone call, riding in an automobile, taking a trip by airplane or ship, swimming or being in the water, visiting the doctor, watching a fire, going to the theater, and being in a confined or underground place. All people living in Western civilization will have these dreams at some time in their lives, and many of them will be repeated again and again.

Let us try to summarize some of the things we have said in this chapter by presenting a few simple figures. A thirty-eight-year-old man kept a record of all the dreams he could recall for one year. During that time, he recorded 103 dreams. In these 103 dreams, there were:

38 dreams that contained at least one aggression
37 dreams that contained at least one misfortune
4 dreams that contained at least one failure
24 dreams that contained at least one friendly act
2 dreams that contained at least one good fortune
7 dreams that contained at least one success
24 dreams that contained at least one sexual act
8 dreams that contained at least one reference to food.

The total number of dreams in which an aggression, misfortune, or failure occurred was 79. The total number of dreams in which a friendly act, good fortune, or success occurred was 33. Six other dream series were analyzed in the same way. The results are brought together in the following table. In reading this table it should be kept in mind that more than one theme can occur in the same dream. That is why the figures in a given column add up to more than the total number of dreams.

	23-yr. old man 100 dreams	32-yr. old man 100 dreams	35-yr. old man 133 dreams	40-yr. old man 113 dreams	56-yr. old man 100 dreams	60-yr. old woman 60 dreams
Number of dreams in which an aggression, misfortune, or failure occurred	54	92	84	97	92	84
Number of dreams in which a friendly act, good fortune, or success occurred	44	25	65	49	55	42
Number of sex dreams	3	22	18	6	2	3
Number of dreams with reference to food or eating	17	8	17	21	17	10

For the seven individuals, who reported a total of 709 dreams, 582 contained an aggression, misfortune, or failure, and 313 contained a friendly act, good fortune, or success. There were 78 sexual and 98 food dreams.

These findings for seven dreamers compare favorably with an analysis of 1000 dreams obtained from 200 young adult males and females. There was an aggression, misfortune, or failure in 931 dreams, and a friendly act, good fortune, or success in 573 dreams.

The conclusion is obvious. Many more bad things than good things happen in dreams. This conclusion is highlighted by the results obtained from an analysis of emotions experienced in dreams. The emotions of sadness, anger, apprehension, and confusion are mentioned 565 times in the 1000 dream reports of young adults. Happy emotions are mentioned only 137 times.

These typical dreams express the shared concerns, preoccupations, and interests of all dreamers. They may be said to constitute the universal constants of the human psyche. To discover and elucidate how they manifest themselves in the dreams of a particular individual, and with what frequency, is one of our primary aims.

Chapter 3

Content Analysis

Content analysis is a method that has been developed to analyze verbal material. To analyze means to break down a verbal report into its constituent elements and count the number of times that each element occurs. The end result of content analysis is a set of frequencies (numbers) for a set of elements. Single elements may be combined to produce classes of elements.

Since dreams are described in words, these verbal reports can be subjected to content analysis. Consider the following dream which was reported by a young man.

My mother was told by my aunt with whom I stay that I had wasted my money buying a book on human anatomy. My mother was very angry, stating how bad it was and how the pictures inside were dirty because they showed naked people. As she was protesting, my father and brothers came to my rescue, stating it was the best thing I ever did. My father said he was proud of me and it showed I was really going to become a great man. The dream ended with my father and brothers siding with me and my mother was left stranded with her own thoughts of the uncleanliness of an anatomy book.

The first set of elements in this dream that attract our attention are the persons involved. These are mother, aunt, father, brothers, naked people, and the dreamer. The dream is primarily about members of the dreamer's family.

The second set of elements consists of interactions between the dreamer and the other persons. The aunt and mother disapprove of the dreamer's purchase of an anatomy book and the father and brothers approve of it. There is no interaction with the naked people who are merely pictures in a book.

The third set of elements are the actions performed by the dream characters. Two types of action are referred to: talking and buying a book.

A fourth set of elements consist of objects. These are money, book, and pictures. A fifth set are the emotions of anger and pride.

Finally, there are several negative and positive value judgments made by the characters: a *bad* book, *dirty* pictures (by mother and aunt) and *best* thing and *great* man (by father).

Obviously, it is not necessary to do such an elaborate analysis of the elements of this dream. The meaning is readily grasped by simply reading the dream. The women of the family are opposed to the dreamer's interest in human anatomy (sex) while the men of the family approve it. The dreamer rejects the feminine values and identifies with the masculine ones. The dream suggests that the young man is having a conflict about his interest in sex, and is trying to resolve it by seeking the support of his father and brothers.

Content analysis is necessary, in fact it is essential, when one has a series or a set of dreams to analyze. In a hundred dreams, for example, there will be numerous characters, objects, and settings, many types of actions and interactions, and a variety of emotions and modifiers. It is impossible to deal with all of this material without resorting to some system of classification.

The frequencies obtained by content analysis tell us what the principal preoccupations of the dreamer are. If, for example, a young man frequently dreams about quarreling with his father, we infer that antagonism between himself and his father weighs heavily upon his mind. If, on the other hand, he rarely dreams about quarreling with his mother, we assume this is not one of his concerns.

The frequencies obtained from a content analysis of an individual's dream series can be compared with the average frequencies obtained from the analysis of a great many series. These average frequencies are called *norms*. By making such a comparison we can tell in what respects a particular dreamer differs from the average or norm. For example, young male Americans dream of failing in 13 out of every

100 dreams. If we analyze an individual's dream series and find he fails 26 times in every 100 dreams, we assume that the dreamer is more preoccupied with failure than the average male of his age is.

After reading thousands of dreams and trying out various systems of classifying the elements in dreams, we finally arrived at one which gave us the information we desired. This system is based solely upon what appears in dreams and is thoroughly objective and simple to use. We will describe the categories and give examples of the use that can be made of them in understanding the dreamer.

Settings

Ordinarily, a dream takes place in an identifiable setting or locale. Settings may be classified in many ways: indoors versus outdoors, familiar versus unfamiliar, realistic versus distorted, recreational versus work, land versus water, and so forth. They may be further subdivided into buildings, streets, lakes, fields, caves, etc. Even finer subclasses are possible: living room, kitchen, bedroom, bathroom, hallway, and porch. It will probably not surprise anyone that the bedroom is one of the most popular of dream settings, or that bed is one of the most frequently appearing objects in dreams.

More dreams take place in familiar settings than unfamiliar ones, although often the familiar setting is more or less distorted from its counterpart in waking life. More dreams occur indoors than outdoors.

There are fairly large differences in the settings dreamed about by men and women. Women dream of being in familiar indoor settings—usually their own houses—more often than men do. Men dream of being out-of-doors more frequently than women do. These differences reflect the differences in the waking life preferences and activities of the two sexes.

The incidence of various types of settings in an individual dream series yields meaningful information about the dreamer. A young man, for example, dreamed much more of being indoors than outdoors. We inferred from this, and from other characteristics of his dreams, that it made him nervous to leave the security and protection of his home and family and venture forth into a strange, cold, and threatening world. What he was really afraid of, it turned out, were his own aggressive and sexual impulses and the risks he ran if they ever broke loose. By remaining indoors, he was able to control these impulses much better.

Another man dreamed repeatedly of his boyhood home in which he had not lived for years and which he rarely visited. From other information obtained from his dreams, we learned that he was dissatisfied with his present life and that he yearned to be a child again.

Objects

The objects that appear in dreams are as many and varied as they are in waking life. We counted over a thousand *different* objects in a thousand dreams. They ranged from accordion to zipper. Objects can be classified into a relatively few categories. The chief ones are:

Architecture: buildings and parts of buildings
Household: furnishings and household articles
Conveyances: automobiles, boats, trains, and elevators
Nature: trees, flowers, rivers, and hills
Clothing: hats, coats, shoes, and dresses
Implements: tools, rope, ladders, and axes.

Each of these categories can have a number of subclasses.

Next to house, the automobile is the most frequently mentioned object in dreams. This is true for Americans who make a fetish of the automobile. We will discuss the meaning of the automobile in dreams in a later chapter.

The frequency with which specific objects are mentioned by an individual dreamer indicates his preferences and preoccupations. In our study of Franz Kafka's dreams, we found many references to clothing. In waking life, he displayed the same preoccupation with clothes. We discovered this preoccupation was motivated by a desire to hide his body, of which he was ashamed. He compensated for feelings of physical inferiority by wearing fashionable clothes.

A businessman sent us 100 of his dreams and asked us to analyze them. His dreams also contained many references to clothes, especially women's clothes. We inferred from this, plus other information secured from his dreams, that he was a transvestite; that is, a person who dresses in the clothes of the opposite sex. This proved to be the case.

In our study of a child molester, several objects were repeatedly mentioned in his dream diary, which turned out to be of considerable importance for understanding his personality. One recurrent object was a printing press. This frequent appearance might not seem strange when it became known that he had worked in a printing establishment. It was observed, however, that the press was often endowed with human characteristics. It played both aggressive and sexual roles in his dreams. Here are some samples of these printing press dreams.

> I wanted to oil a printing press. A man was sitting on the press. He said to pour the oil into his mouth through a funnel. I did so, and he became ill.

> I was repairing a printing press that had something dangling from it.

> I was behind a printing press against the wall. The press started up and began to open. When the press was completely opened it would be so close to the wall that it would crush me. I awoke as the press was pressing me against the wall and crushing me. I was terrified.

He also dreamed frequently of holes. This obsession with holes was related to his pathological interest in the female genitals. Much of his child-molesting consisted of looking at, or trying to look at, the genitals of little girls. He was also a compulsive Peeping Tom. He could not or did not want to believe that women lacked penises, because if they did, it meant there was a possibility he could lose his. Consequently, he was continually searching for the missing penis of the woman. In some of his dreams, he even endowed women with the external organs of the male.

In a dream series provided by a male schoolteacher we shall call Tony, houses played a prominent role. They were pictured in his dreams as being old, dilapidated, crumbling, in ruins, or in need of repair. When Tony was asked to say what houses meant to him, he replied with these comments. "It was some time before I realized that houses played an important part in my dreams. I think the house must be me, more specifically, my body or my mind." The dreamer felt he was growing old and rundown physically. He was particularly concerned about his failing sexual potency and his virility as a male. It is interesting that in waking life Tony bought old houses and restored them.

A person often chooses a hobby or a vocation in order to overcome his doubts and fears about himself. Mountain climbers frequently dream of falling, which indicated to us that they were trying to overcome a fear of high places by choosing climbing as an avocation. The same high incidence of accidents was found in the dreams of a surfer. Another dreamer who was a body builder in waking life dreamed of other men who had better bodies than his. This suggested to us that his interest in physical culture was an attempt to overcome doubts about his own virility.

Body Parts

References to parts of the body are common in dreams. They are classified under five headings.

Head: visible body parts above the shoulders
Extremities: arms and legs
Torso: all visible parts from the shoulders to the hips
Anatomy: internal organs and body secretions
Sexual: body parts and organs related to reproduction and excretion

The child molester had numerous dreams in which references were made to internal organs and the genitals, unlike most dreamers who dream more often of the extremities and the head. He was preoccupied with sex and with the inside of the body. He wanted to get inside the body to explore its mysteries and to find protection from the outside world. His dreams also had many indoor settings. This return-to-the-womb motif expressed itself in other ways: by dreaming about entering or being in caves, tunnels, shafts, sewers, holes, and other subterranean places, and by dreams of swimming.

Swimming was his favorite and only form of physical recreation in waking life. Here is one of his swimming dreams in which a return-to-the-womb theme is suggested.

I was swimming in a pool. I made large bubbles by clapping my hands in the water. One was big enough for me to get inside. It felt like plastic. I prepared to get inside the bubble.

He spent many years in confinement. When he was not in an institution he lived with his mother and sister and had few contacts with other people. The reverse side of the coin is that when he was in confinement he often dreamed of breaking out through holes. The womblike, fetal existence was too confining and had its own special dangers for him.

One of the clues that helped us to a better understanding of Franz Kafka was the high incidence of references to body parts. These references occurred not only in his dreams but also in his diaries. In many of the dreams a part of the body was disfigured or defective. This suggested an aversion to his body and also to other bodies. This aversion proved to be a serious obstacle to his happiness. It was one of the reasons he never married, abhorred sex, and finally contracted tuberculosis from which he died. He confessed in his diary that he had physically destroyed himself by the way in which he lived.

Characters

A dream usually has several characters in addition to the dreamer. These characters may be classified by sex, age, occupation, ethnic background, prominence, and relationship to the dreamer. Familiar persons may be differentiated from strangers, individuals from groups, and animals from humans. Family members may be subdivided into mother, father, brother, sister, wife, husband, son, and daughter.

The cast of dream characters is a lengthy one. One person who recorded 308 dreams over a five-year period dreamed about 343 *different* characters. The persons we dream about most frequently are those with whom we have the closest relationship in waking life. Husbands dream about wives, and wives about husbands. Parents dream about their children, and their children dream about them. Lovers dream about each other, and so do close friends.

The person who had 343 different characters in his 308 dreams dreamed repeatedly about a few people. His wife appeared in 33 dreams (the highest frequency), his daughter in 11 dreams, and his mother and father (who had been dead for years) in seven dreams and four dreams, respectively. Three of his best friends appeared in 14, 15, and 17 dreams. The frequency with which these characters appeared was a fairly accurate measure of the intensity of the relationship he had with them. With a few exceptions, when a relationship with a person weakens or is broken through death, separation, or loss of interest, that person disappears from one's dreams. The exceptions are the dreamer's mother and father and his spouse. These individuals never seem to vanish completely.

An elderly woman who had been married twice and whose

husbands had been dead for years continued to dream about both of them for the rest of her life. Her first marriage was an unhappy one which ended in divorce. Life with her second husband was much happier. His death left her grief-stricken and desolate. When the dreams about her two husbands were analyzed and compared, a surprising difference in the way in which they appeared in her dreams was clearly evident.

In many of the dreams of her first husband, they were having a good time together, often in an amorous manner. In no instance did she relive in her dreams the bad times she had with him during their marriage. By contrast, the majority of dreams involving her second husband were distinctly unpleasant. He was seen as sick and dying or leaving her for another woman. She would dream of being with him, then he would disappear and she could not find him.

As noted earlier, a person tends to dream recurrently of a traumatic experience in an attempt to overcome the tremendous amount of anxiety produced by the experience. Thirty-six years after the death of her second husband, she was still reliving the experience in her dreams. This indicates she had still not mastered her shock and grief. If dreams were kinder, if they were simple wish fulfillments or compensated for the frustrations of waking life, she should have dreamed more often of his being alive and well. In fact, as the years passed, she had fewer such dreams and more dreams of separation, loss, and desertion.

One could argue that by dreaming of his loss, by separation or death, she was trying to accustom herself to the painful reality of his death. "He really is dead" is the message that her dreams were trying to get across to her. If this were the case, the message had to be repeated over and over again because it never had a permanent effect. The dreamer herself commented on the cruelty of these recurrent dreams in which her second husband was taken away from her over and over again.

She was also perplexed by the happy dreams in which she was reunited with her first husband. If the first husband had been alive while she was having these dreams of him, they might be explained as being compensatory. She could be saying, "Since my second husband is irretrievably dead, the only possible compensation for my grief is to return to my first husband." But the first husband had also been dead for years. Since both husbands were equally dead, why did she not relive the very satisfying experiences with her second husband? Apparently, her first love had a stronger hold on her than she was willing to admit in waking life.

The following dream, reported to us when the dreamer was 82 years old, describes the dilemma she has lived with for fifty years.

> Two men were in love with me and wanted me to marry them. One was quiet and high-minded and altogether a far nicer, modest person. The other was handsome and flamboyant and took me by storm, simply assuming my consent. I wasn't exactly in love with either, but fascinated and overcome by the second man, and I did say yes and married him, though even then I doubted if I was making the better choice. Then when it was too late I realized what a mistake I had made; my husband was self-centered and arrogant, and once he had me, he treated me with indifference.

The quiet, high-minded man was like her second husband; the flamboyant one was like her first husband. She still shows her preference for the first one, mistaken though she feels she may be.

Another elderly woman who had not been married had recurring dreams about her mother at a rate of about one in every ten dreams. She rarely dreamed about her father, who had died when she was a young child.

The pattern of relationships that a person has in his waking life is divulged in his dreams, as the following example illustrates. A woman who has been sending us her dreams for years dreamed about the following persons:

husband	134 times
sister X	110 times
daughter	103 times
male supervisor	83 times
sister Y	53 times
mother	51 times
brother	8 times
father	twice

Although she saw a great deal of both sisters, who lived together, her feelings about sister X were more complicated and intense than were those about sister Y. She rarely saw her brother, who lived in a distant city, and her father died when she was nine years old. She was very close to her mother, whom she visited daily until the mother died. She continued to dream about her mother even more so after her death. She was also very close to her daughter. It was evident from her dreams that she was in love with her supervisor. It was her husband, however, that she dreamed about most frequently. We will have more to say about her relations with these people later.

The presence of a large number of strangers in dreams suggests that the dreamer is isolated from people. This was certainly the case with the child molester, who rarely dreamed about anyone he knew except for his mother and sister with whom he lived. He never had any real friends, even as a boy, in part because his mother frowned upon it, and in part because of his eccentric behavior.

When one classifies strangers by sex it is found that many more of them are males than females. As we have already seen in Chapter 2, the prototype for the male stranger in many dreams is the father.

There is an interesting and virtually universal difference in the frequency with which males and females dream about other males and females. Male dreamers dream more often about other males than they do about females. The ratio is about two males to one female. Females dream about males and females in equal proportions. This difference has been observed in children as well as in adults, and in various ethnic and nationality groups.

When we break down the characters by sex into family members, relatives, known persons, and strangers, the sex difference is as follows. Male and female family members appear equally often in the dreams of males (57 males versus 56 females) whereas female family members and relatives outnumber males in the dreams of females (99 males versus 135 females). Male dreamers dream more often about male friends than female friends (204 males versus 117 females) and female dreamers dream more often about female friends than male friends (192 males versus 249 females). Male strangers predominate over female strangers in the dreams of both sexes, but the difference is larger for male dreamers (301 males versus 107 females) than for female dreamers (196 males versus 148 females). These figures were taken from dreamers in their late teens and early twenties, and most of them were not married.

What all of these facts indicate is that the male is *much* more preoccupied with other males, except for family members and relatives, than he is with females. The female is *slightly* more preoccupied with other females, except for strangers, than she is with males.

Prominent Persons

A prominent person is defined as a well-known individual who appears in one's dreams. The individual may be a real person either living or dead, a supernatural being, or a fictional character. Below are listed the prominent persons appearing in two dream series, one reported by a woman in her sixties, the other by a man in his fifties.

FEMALE SERIES

Chester (a character in the TV series *Gunsmoke*)
Montgomery Clift (actor)
Sammy Davis, Jr. (entertainer)
Queen Elizabeth
Ella Fitzgerald (singer)
Stewart Granger (actor)
William Holden (actor)
Audrey Hepburn (actress)
Glenn Ford (actor)
Ernest Hemingway (writer)
Vaughn Monroe (singer)
Deborah Kerr (actress)
Steve McQueen (actor)
Gregory Peck (actor)
Prince Philip
Mickey Rooney (actor)
John D. Rockefeller (businessman)
Robert Preston (actor)
Frank Sinatra (entertainer)

MALE SERIES

Dean Acheson (politician)
A. A. Brill (psychoanalyst)
John F. Byrnes (politician)
John Ciardi (poet)
Doris Day (actress)
John Foster Dulles (politician)
President Dwight D. Eisenhower
Sigmund Freud (psychoanalyst)
President John F. Kennedy
Evelyn McLean (society leader)
Margaret Mead (anthropologist)
President Richard M. Nixon
Charles Norris (writer)
The Pope
Governor Nelson Rockefeller
Premier Josef Stalin
George Szell (conductor)
Henry Wallace (politician)
President Woodrow Wilson

It will be observed that the two lists are very different. The woman dreams primarily about film stars and entertainers; the man dreams primarily about politicians and intellectuals. The two lists accurately reflect the interests of the two dreamers. One often watches late movies before going to sleep; the other is more apt to be listening to current events or music, or reading books before retiring.

One of our dreamers had many more dreams of prominent people than the average dreamer of his age and sex has. This high frequency was related to his own desire to be a well-known person. Another dreamer often dreamed of a well-known admiral. It was apparent from the dreams that the admiral served as a father-substitute for the dreamer. The dreamer did not admire his own father but he did admire the admiral.

Animals

The subject of animals in dreams is so fascinating that it warrants a book by itself. Much of the fascination results from the obvious symbolic role that animals play in dreams. They are said to represent, as discussed in Chapter 2, the instincts or animal impulses (Freud) or the shadow side of personality (Jung). They often chase or attack the dreamer, causing him to awaken in agonizing terror. They may also represent the bad or punitive father or mother.

The list of animals that appear in dreams is as varied as a menagerie. Here, for example, are the different animals that appeared in the dreams of an older woman:

WILD MAMMALS

grizzly bear
trained bear
chimpanzee
cheetah
deer
lion
opossum
panther

DOMESTIC MAMMALS

cat
dog
hamster
horse
pig

BIRDS

bluejay
canary
owl
rooster

INSECTS, REPTILES, ETC.

ant
caterpillar
flea
frog
grasshopper
slug
snail
snake
spider
toad
worm

SEA ANIMALS, FISH

barnacles
goldfish
jelly fish
lobster
oyster
salmon
turtle
walrus

The most frequently appearing animal was the cat, an animal of which the dreamer was especially fond, having two of her own. The dog, another favorite animal, was next most frequent, followed by slugs and snails which she hated because they caused so much damage to her garden. Loving cats and hating snails explains their high frequency in her dreams. She had very intense emotions associated with these animals in waking life; thus, the high preoccupation with them in dreams. All of the other animals listed appeared less frequently in her dreams, because her emotions associated with them were less intense.

Children dream much more about animals than adults do. This interest in animals is sometimes attributed to the animal stories children are read, often just before they go to sleep. It is also possible, and in our eyes more probable, that children prefer stories about animals because they dramatize their own wishes and fears.

People living close to nature (so-called primitive people) continue to dream about animals with great frequency throughout their lives. Animals appear in 50 percent of the dreams reported by adult Yir Yoront, a tribe of Australian aborigines. This percentage is equivalent to the percentage of animal dreams reported by American children, ages four to five. Folklore and mythology throughout the world are filled with animals.

Interactions

The three most frequent and significant types of interactions between the dreamer and other characters are aggression, friendliness, and sex. Aggression expresses itself in many ways, from mild feelings of hostility to murder. The two most common forms of aggression in dreams are chasing-attacking and quarrels-admonitions. One is physical, the other verbal. Men have more physical aggressions and women have more verbal aggressions in their dreams just as they do in waking life. The two most common forms of friendliness are doing something for a person and a friendly greeting or compliment. Sexual interactions run the gamut from fondling to sexual intercourse.

An analysis of the types of interactions which the dreamer has with various classes of characters reveals some interesting sex differences and individual differences. For example, male dreamers have more aggressive encounters with males than with females. And males have more friendliness and of course more sexual encounters with females than with males. This ties in nicely with Freud's theory of the Oedipus complex, which states that the boy's positive feelings for his mother and his negative feelings for his father influence his subsequent feelings toward males and females. Actually, the theory states that he has mixed or ambivalent feelings toward both parents, and that positive and negative are only a matter of degree. This same ambivalence is found in dreams, as we shall see.

It is ironic that the discoverer of the Oedipus complex should himself have had an inverted complex. Freud had more aggression with females than with males, and more friendly encounters with males than with females in his dreams. Jung, who became critical of Freudian theory, had a more normal pattern of interactions with males and females in his dreams. This difference between the two men may have been responsible in part for the breakdown in their association, which originally had been very close.

Female dreamers are equally aggressive and equally

friendly with males and females, although they are more aggressive and more friendly with males than they are with females. These findings also agree with the female version of the Oedipus complex, which states that the little girl has a mixture of negative and positive feelings toward both parents which carries over into later life. In other words, the female is just *more* ambivalent than the male is about her relations with people. This ambivalence is very important, we feel, for understanding the psychology of women.

Ambivalence, or mixed feelings of friendliness and hostility for the same person, comes to light when we examine the interactions of a dreamer with specific persons in his dreams. For example, the woman mentioned earlier who had numerous dreams about her husband, daughter, mother, two sisters, and supervisor showed the following pattern of aggressive and friendly interactions with each of them.

Husband:	66 aggressive and 47 friendly interactions
Sister X:	41 aggressive and 43 friendly interactions
Daughter:	25 aggressive and 58 friendly interactions
Supervisor:	42 aggressive and 61 friendly interactions
Sister Y:	10 aggressive and 7 friendly interactions
Mother:	4 aggressive and 30 friendly interactions

She was most ambivalent about her two sisters, and least ambivalent about her mother and daughter. Negative feelings predominate toward her husband, and positive ones toward her supervisor. She acknowledged that this is the way she feels toward them in waking life.

Ambivalence of feeling toward major characters has been found in every dream series we have examined. The important differentiating factor is the relative amount of aggression and friendliness toward specific characters or classes of characters. Male dreamers are most ambivalent toward male characters they know (57 aggressive versus 55 friendly), more negative toward male strangers (108 aggressive versus 42 friendly), and more positive toward known females (29 aggressive versus 52 friendly). They have slightly more friendly than aggressive interactions with female strangers (21 aggressive versus 32 friendly).

Female dreamers are most ambivalent toward known female characters (58 aggressive versus 53 friendly), more negative toward male strangers (52 aggressive versus 31 friendly), and more positive toward known males (60 aggressive versus 90 friendly). Like male dreamers, they have slightly more friendly than aggressive encounters with female strangers (20 aggressive versus 27 friendly).

Male strangers are cast in the role of enemies more often than friends for both sexes. Otherwise, the rule is ambivalence toward known characters of the same sex as the dreamer, and a preponderance of positive feelings toward known characters of the opposite sex. These findings are in agreement with the Oedipus complex theory. It will be observed, however, that female dreamers are neither as strongly positive nor as strongly negative in their feelings as male dreamers are. Females tend to be more ambivalent toward all classes of characters which is also what the Oedipus complex states.

One group of characters that are clearly perceived as being enemies for both sexes are animals. There are few friendly interactions with them.

An aggressive interaction customarily has an aggressor, the one who initiates the aggression, and a victim. In all *sets* of dreams that we have analyzed the dreamer is more often the victim than he is the aggressor. The incidence of being a victim is higher in children's dreams and adult female dreams. In some individual cases, however, the dreamer is more often the aggressor. Moreover, there are differences in the frequency with which the dreamer is the victim both for specific characters or groups of characters.

Male and female dreamers are more likely to be aggressed against both by known males and male strangers than by female characters. There is, however, a sex difference in the incidence of being a victim. Male dreamers receive more aggression from male strangers than from known males. Female dreamers are the victim of aggression from known males and male strangers about the same amount of time. Both sexes give and receive aggression about equally often with all female characters.

The male stranger, as pointed out in Chapter 2, turns out to be the chief threat for both sexes. Females bear the additional burden of being threatened by familiar males. They are also more threatened by animals than males are.

It is interesting to speculate how much, if any, of the woman's fear of being attacked represents a fear of being sexually assaulted. Rape fantasies are not uncommon among women, and dreams of being raped have been reported by them. The fact that they are so often attacked by familiar males suggests that the attack may represent, in some cases, a symbolic sexual assault. By the same token, men's dreams of attacking women may symbolize a sexual attack.

Actions

The dreamer or another character may engage in activities that do not require interacting with others. He may walk, drive a car, ride a bicycle, sail, or ski. He may think, read, or write. He may repair a tire, operate a machine, play the piano, eat, drink, shave, or wash his hair. He may laugh or cry. In fact, he may do anything he does during waking life plus some things he cannot do, such as flying by waving his arms. Activities can be classified into a small number of categories: physical, movement, verbal, expressive (for instance, laughing), seeing, hearing, and thinking.

By and large, a person dreams about those activities that interest him in waking life. He is more apt to dream about his hobbies than he is about his regular work or chores. A businessman whose dreams we analyzed rarely dreamed about his job—in fact, it was impossible to tell what kind of work he did from his dreams—but he frequently dreamed about stamp-collecting activities, which was his ardent pastime. The Mount Everest climbers had numerous dreams about climbing mountains, and not just the one they were climbing while they were reporting their dreams. A sports car enthusiast dreamed repeatedly about sports cars. Men, as might be expected, have more physical activities in their dreams than women do.

Analysis of activities may shed light upon important features of the dreamer's personality. Kafka, for instance, was a watcher rather than a doer in his dreams. He was both voyeuristic and passive in his dreams, as he was also in waking life.

One of our dreamers, a young man, was an avid surfer who never missed an opportunity to engage in his favorite pastime. He lived and breathed surfing. He also dreamed it. Of the 300 dreams recorded in his dream diary, which was kept for a year and a half, 55 made some reference to surfing.

Preoccupied with surfing as he was during the day, it might be thought that he would be performing feats of surfing in his sleep. Such was not the case. He was seldom surfing in his dreams. Most of the time he was on land watching the waves or watching others surf. When he was not watching waves or surfers, he was talking about surfing or looking at pictures of surfing. Thirty-five of the dreams fell into this passive and voyeuristic category.

In the remaining 20 dreams, he was (1) paddling on his board but not surfing, (2) prevented from going surfing by an obstacle, (3) unable to catch a wave, (4) losing his board, or (5) having a mishap while surfing. In only four dreams was he surfing without mishap or frustration. No feats of skill or complicated maneuvers were performed in these four dreams.

No simple wish-fulfillment theory can explain these dreams. What they suggest is that the dreamer plays a passive role with respect to his favorite sport. In his dreams, surfing is a spectator sport. He stands on land and looks out to sea where the waves are breaking and others are riding them, without risk to himself. When he attempts to participate more actively, he encounters an obstacle or has a mishap. The dreams intimate that his feelings about surfing may be more ambivalent than he cares to recognize or admit. We saw the same ambivalence expressed in dreams reported by mountain climbers. Perhaps all forms of strong attachments, whether they be attachments to objects, activities, or persons, possess the oppositional qualities of attraction and repulsion.

Success and Failure

The dreamer may succeed or fail in whatever task he sets out to perform. Success and failure occur about equally often in dreams. Women succeed *and* fail in their dreams less often than men do. This suggests that women may be less achievement-oriented.

Individual dreamers may deviate from these norms. Kafka experienced less success in his dreams, which is congruent with his inferiority feelings in waking life. He thought of himself as a failure. Freud, on the other hand, had much more success than failure in his dreams. *He* never suffered from an inferiority complex.

Misfortune and Good Fortune

A misfortune is anything bad that happens to a dreamer or a character over which he has no control, and which is not the result of an intentional act of aggression by someone else. Misfortunes can be divided into six classes: death, injury or illness, accident or destruction of property, a threat by something in the environment other than a person or an animal, falling, and frustration. Good fortune is the opposite of misfortune. It occurs so rarely in dreams that it is not necessary to have separate classes of good fortune. As we said in Chapter 2, misfortunes outnumber good fortunes by six to one.

Differences in the number of misfortunes or good fortunes do occur in individual dream series. Freud, who had many successes in his dreams, had no good fortunes at all. Jung, with an average number of successes, had a lot of good fortunes. Jung was much more fatalistic about his life than Freud was. He was inclined to let things happen to him, to let his life be lived rather than to live it. His life, he said, "developed naturally and by destiny." Near the end of his life Jung wrote, "Today I can say it is truly astounding that I have had as much success as has been accorded me."

Emotions

It is surprising to us who have read and analyzed thousands of dreams that more emotions are not experienced by the dreamer. The nightmare or anxiety dream in which the dreamer experiences such intense emotion that it awakens him is an exception to this statement. There are many dreams that *should* produce fear, anger, grief, or joy that do not. A person may undergo a grueling set of experiences while he is dreaming and remain emotionally indifferent. One dreamer, for example, had dreams in which he was in danger of drowning, engaged in passionate lovemaking, watching people being burned at the stake, preparing to fight off an invading army, and fleeing from a forest fire. In none of these dreams did he feel any emotion. We have not been able to understand why events that cause strong emotional reactions in waking life do not do the same in dreams.

Enough emotions are felt, however, to warrant making a classification of them. Five classes suffice: happiness, anger, apprehension (fear), sadness, and confusion. The unpleasant emotions of sadness, anger, apprehension, and confusion outnumber happy emotions by more than four to one. Apprehension, including anxiety and guilt, is the most commonly felt emotion, and sadness the least common. Women experience more emotion in their dreams than men do.

Modifiers

Objects, characters, and activities may be described as having certain attributes. "It was a *red* automobile." "The room was *empty*." "It was a *hot* day." "She was very *homely*." "I walked *slowly*." One could make an extensive classification of these adjectives and adverbs, but we have limited the number of categories to the nine most frequently used ones in dream reports. These are color, size, intensity, linearity (straight, curved, or crooked), thermal (hot and cold), velocity, age (young or old), and evaluative (pretty-ugly and good-bad).

Intensity and size are the most commonly used classes of modifiers. Strong and large far exceed weak and small in frequency of usage, and positive evaluations exceed negative ones.

There are some interesting sex differences. Women dream more about color but less about size than men do. They also make more value judgments, both favorable and unfavorable, than men do. Men dream more about rapid movement than women do. In their dreams, men are driving automobiles fast or they are in a speeding boat, or they are running fast. In waking life, men probably engage in more rapid movement than women do.

In individual dream series, an unusual number of modifiers of a particular class may point to important characteristics of the dreamer. One man whose dreams we analyzed had a large number of negative evaluations. The world for him was more ugly and bad than it was beautiful and good. This suggested to us he might have a misanthropic attitude toward life which proved to be true.

This completes our description of content analysis as applied to dreams. Several comments are in order. The first one is that the system we have devised can be expanded or contracted to accommodate itself to the aims of a particular study. It is not necessary to adhere strictly to the system. We do not hesitate to devise new categories for a particular dream series when they are required. The system should not be used in a mechanical fashion. It is an aid to understanding dreams and dreamers, and a necessity when one is analyzing large numbers of dreams, but it does not unlock doors to new knowledge without intelligent participation by the analyst.

One rarely knows beforehand which categories are going

to be the most informative about the dreamer. That is why we employ a broad system of classification. For one dream series, a particular modifier may provide an important clue; for another it may be the distribution of characters or the presence of certain objects or the types of activities in which the dreamer engages.

An advantage of using a broad system of classification is illustrated by a study we did on the dreams of various types of male mental patients. We found only a few differences among the different types. Alcoholics had more dreams in which there was a reference to eating or drinking, which is scarcely a world-shaking revelation. We then took all of the patient dreams and compared them with the dreams of a non-patient population. To our astonishment, there were very few differences. We doubt that anyone could distinguish patient dreams from normal dreams just by reading them. The differences that content analysis did reveal, however, were of crucial psychological importance. They centered around the dreamer's aggressive and friendly interactions with female characters. The normal male dreamer has more friendly than aggressive encounters with women. In patient dreams, this was reversed; they had more aggressive than friendly interactions with females.

In interpreting this finding, we suggested that their hostility toward women stemmed from early childhood experiences of being rejected by the mother. A child who feels rejected is more vulnerable to threats from the external world and from his own impulses. His character is weakened so that he is more likely to collapse when under pressure. The breakdown may take many forms. He may become overly anxious (neurotic), he may try to drown his anxiety in alcohol, he may suffer from any one of a variety of psychosomatic disorders, he may flee into a fantasy world (schizophrenia), or he may destroy himself (suicide).

We have mentioned before that using the method of content analysis of reported dreams enables the dream to be taken out of the psychiatrist's consulting room and into the larger world. We would like to point out now that this method can be used advantageously within the psychiatric setting as well.

A study was made by a psychologist of 61 dreams reported by a young woman during her 32 months of psychotherapy. He attempted to uncover her principal conflicts and concerns. His approach to the dreams was very subjective and impressionistic, so that the resulting picture of the patient was blurred, confused, and chaotic.

We subjected the dreams to the method of content analysis described in this chapter, and discovered that her primary concerns were as follows: men, sex, marriage and divorce, pregnancy, birth control, and abortion; filth; implements; misfortune; anxiety; and money. The dreams about money were related to the lengthy discussions of the payment of fees between the psychotherapist and the patient. The other items suggested to us that what the patient wanted was a husband and babies, but she was afraid of having her body invaded, dirtied, and destroyed by the act of intercourse and pregnancy. Menstruation was a monthly reminder to her of the uncleanliness of the genital regions. Had the psychotherapist focused on her paralyzing fears of body destruction, he might have shortened the length of treatment and increased its effectiveness.

What content analysis does—and it is all that it does—is to provide frequencies of occurrence for a large number of dream elements. From these frequencies inferences are drawn which can then be checked against other evidence.

Throughout this chapter we have assumed that the frequency with which someone or something is dreamed about is in direct proportion with the dreamer's preoccupation, concern, or interest. If a husband dreams more often about his wife than any other person, we can be quite certain that his wife is the most important person in his present life. In what way she is important to him can be determined by analyzing the types of interactions he has with her in his dreams. If a young woman dreams more about riding horseback than any other form of recreation, we do not have to be told that she does a lot of riding in waking life. If a dreamer has a great many sex dreams we are sure to find he is also preoccupied with sex when he is awake.

This rule occasionally breaks down. The child molester who never dreamed about his father is an example. We have never found a case where a person dreamed a great deal about someone or something in which he was not interested or with which he was not concerned in some way.

We have also used two other methods of analysis. They are *theoretical categories* and *contingency analysis*.

Theoretical Categories

The categories or classes of elements that have been described in this chapter are said to be empirical ones because they occur directly in dream reports. There is nothing inferential or theoretical about settings, objects, characters, interactions, and so forth. It is possible, however, to devise classes that are theoretical. A theoretical category is one that is taken from a theory of personality.

According to Freudian theory, for example, the child passes through several stages, each of which is associated with a pleasure-arousing (erogenous) part of the body. During the first stage, the baby obtains pleasure from stimulation of its mouth; during the second stage pleasure from stimulation of the anal region; and during the third stage pleasure from stimulation of the genitals. Each of these makes a contribution to the personality development of the individual, but the amount contributed by each stage varies from person to person. One person may be more oral, another more anal, and a third more phallic in his behavior.

If we wish to assess the strength of each of these vectors from an analysis of dreams, it is necessary to formulate categories that define orality, anality, and the phallic stage. Let us use orality to illustrate what is meant by a theoretical category. The classes of elements in dreams that indicate orality are the following ones:

1. Eating and drinking
2. Being in an eating place
3. Preparing food
4. Obtaining food by buying it or picking it
5. Any mention of food

We can now go through a dream series and count the number of times each of these elements is mentioned. A person whose dreams contain a large number of references to these elements is said to be an oral character. This inference can then be checked against other evidence to see whether it is correct.

It will be noted that what we have done to establish a theoretical category is to pick out a group of empirical elements and call them by the name of a theoretical concept. There are no theoretical elements as such in dreams; there are only empirical elements that can be subsumed under a theoretical label.

One of our dreamers, an older woman, had many dreams of food and eating. We chose fifty of these dreams in order to see how the oral elements were represented. There were many more dreams in which she was preparing food for other people than dreams in which food was being prepared for her. That is, her dreams showed that she was more nurturing of others than dependent upon them. In some of the nurturing dreams she was irritated by having to serve others, or refused to serve them.

In many of the dreams, food was associated with messiness. Food was spilled or spoiled, or the kitchen or restaurant was untidy. In several dreams, the dreamer passed gas while she was eating or had bad breath from eating. In one dream, she was sitting on the toilet gorging herself with ice cream. In another, food had been placed in her dresser drawer and was infested with insects.

There was also a large number of frustrating oral dreams. She was not waited on, she received small portions or spoiled food, the meal was delayed or interrupted, or the restaurant was closed. There were only a few dreams in which the dreamer was eating a meal in a normal and satisfying manner.

Her most unusual oral dream was one in which she and her two sisters were eating their own flesh.

We were eating the flesh from our faces. We all looked like skulls. One of my sisters had taken her nose off already. My other sister and I wished she would have waited with that until last because she looked so awful.

This analysis shows that the dreamer was preoccupied with food in her dreams, but she was not an oral character in the Freudian sense of being a dependent, demanding, greedy person. Her oral preoccupations were usually distasteful or frustrating in character. The messiness suggests elimination rather than eating.

Two conditions in her life may have helped to form these negative feelings about food. From the age of ten to eighteen, she lived in an orphanage. During one period when the matron was behaving irrationally, the children did not get enough to eat and the food was filthy. When she married, her husband had eccentric eating habits which she had to cater to. Most of the time he ate creamy soups, softboiled eggs, malted milkshakes, and other (messy?) foods. He was also concerned about his elimination and often took enemas (more messiness?). Naturally, his wife felt resentful.

Her associations with food are not pleasant either in her dreams or in waking life. The dreamer is a moderate eater, prefers plain food, has kept the same weight for years, seldom drinks, has never smoked, and does not like to cook.

Contingency Analysis

Content analysis has been criticized because it breaks a dream into fragments, thereby destroying the unity and coherence of the dream. This objection can be overcome in several ways. One method consists of combining the elements obtained by content analysis to form constellations of elements. For example, in studying aggression in dreams, we take into account not only the type of aggression but also the identities of the characters who are involved in the interaction, the character who initiates the aggression, the character who is the victim, and the reaction of the victim. To this complex of elements can also be added the events that led up to the aggression, the consequences of the aggression, the feelings and emotions of the combatants, the setting in which the aggression took place, and the objects used in the aggression. In other words, after a dream has been broken down into its elements it can be reassembled again.

Another method of showing relationships among dream elements is *contingency analysis*. This method of statistical comparison enables the investigator to determine what elements occur together more often than would be expected by chance on the basis of a random sample. For example, it has been observed by content analysis that whenever an animal appears in a certain child's dream, the same dream is also likely to contain the elements of fear and aggression. In one dream series that we analyzed, it was found that many of the dreams in which the dreamer, a male, engaged in sexual activity also contained the element of being interrupted by a third person—usually an older woman—which resulted in the dreamer feeling embarrassed and guilty.

Here is another example of the application of contingency analysis to dreams. Around the turn of the century, a young Bostonian kept a record of his dreams for several years. His diary was later published in a book on dreams. Upon reading this diary, we were struck by a group of items that recurred throughout the 84 dreams. There were references to tunnels and pipes, rear or end, pressure or tightness, dirty, odor, brown, noise, water, trains, boats, rocks, something removed, and empty. When a contingency analysis was made of these items, it was found that they were associated with one another more often than would be expected by chance. They formed a complex of experiences that we inferred were associated with the eliminative processes and organs of the body. *Pressure* and *noise* refer to the act of elimination, and *pipe* and *rear* to the anatomical structures by which the act is performed. *Brown* is the color of feces, which are *dirty* and *smelly*. Feces are like *stones,* or *boats* submerged in *water,* or *train* cars coupled together. By the act of defecation something is *removed* from the body, and after it is completed, there is a feeling of *emptiness*. The dreamer was apparently preoccupied with his own eliminative functions.

The following dream sums up the focal point of his preoccupations.

I walked repeatedly through a *stone arched railway culvert*. It was not the celebrated one at 'Ame *Pratts*'. Each time I went in below and crawled out by a vertical *shaft* on the other side of the track. Toward morning I found myself reduced to about six inches tall and once more in an underground place. It was a *cubical chamber* about as big as a soapbox. The circular *tunnels* slanted away toward the surface of the earth and through them a pinkish light streamed. I was in the *burrow* of a white rabbit that soon appeared. He seemed quite peaceable but his comparatively enormous size made me uneasy. He was in fact nearly two feet long. I started out by one of the *tunnels,* walking backwards. The rabbit followed, also backing. I pounded his *flanks* with my puny fists but with no effect. Emerging from the *hole* I suddenly regained my normal size, captured the rabbit, and carried him off. He was now *brown*. I thought I must kill him for the laboratory but I was very unwilling. Finally I tried to strangle him with one hand while with the other I felt his warm chest to note when his heart should stop beating. But my resolution failed and I let the poor animal revive. I carried him through Newtonville Square and came to a *decaying colonial* house.

Obviously, this dream contains psychosexual material other than the anal references which have been italicized. There is the return to the womb and rebirth fantasy. This fantasy, however, is linked to the anal complex by virtue of the fact that children often think that babies are born through the anus. They equate the act of defecation with birth.

Content analysis used in conjuction with contingency analysis is a powerful tool in dream research. It enables the investigator to uncover a network of associated items in dreams which might otherwise be overlooked.

Chapter *4*

Symbols in Dreams

For a large majority of dreams, a simple analysis of the dreamer's interactions with persons, animals, and objects can tell us a great deal about the dreamer. No other information is necessary except the dreams themselves. In order to perform this type of objective analysis for an individual dream series, a fairly large number of dreams is desirable.

Sometimes, however, it is useful and revealing to treat an element of a dream as a symbol that represents something else. This something else we call a *referent*. The symbol has to be deciphered in order to discover what it refers to and thus arrive at a correct interpretation of the dream.

In ancient times, the decoding of symbols was performed by professional dream interpreters, or by consulting dream books that listed symbolic elements in dreams and their referents. Official dream interpreters still exist in many parts of the world today, and dream books are available in bookstores and libraries. There are also psychoanalytical dream books that explain the meanings of various symbols.

In this chapter we shall discuss some of the modern methods that have been devised for decoding symbols. First, we should define what is meant by a symbol. As we have said, a symbol is something that stands in place of something else. Words are symbols because they denote objects, actions, qualities, feelings, and many other things. Numbers are symbols because they stand for quantities. This type of symbol is *representational* or *denotative* in character. The denotative symbol is not what one has in mind when he speaks of dream symbolism.

The symbols that appear in dreams are *metaphorical*. A metaphorical symbol is one that stands for something other than what it appears to be. When one says black is a symbol of death, white is a symbol of purity, and red is a symbol of passion, one is speaking in metaphors. When one says a gun in a dream is not a gun but a penis, or a cave is not a cave but a vagina, one is also speaking in metaphors.

Metaphor is employed when we wish to convey a meaning, a feeling, a conception, or an attitude about something. If a man says of a woman, "You are the apple of my eye," and she replies, "And you are my tower of strength," we have a pretty good idea of how they feel about each other.

Metaphor is particularly useful when we wish to express a complex of meanings and feelings by a simple, economical expression or image. When a woman exclaims to the man she loves, "You are my sun," she expresses a number of conceptions. Sun can mean at one and the same time "you are the light of my life," "you fill me with warmth," "you are exalted in my eyes," and "you are the center around which my life revolves."

Black as a symbol of death conveys a complex of qualities, among them invisibility, inscrutability, blankness, impenetrability, unconsciousness, disappearance, nothingness, gloom, evil, and dread. Such a complex of meanings constitutes a conceptual system. "All the world's a stage" tells us in a single word what the world meant to Hamlet. On another occasion, Hamlet felt the world was a sterile promontory. These two metaphors, "stage" and "sterile promontory," express quite different thoughts and feelings. Metaphor is the language of poetry, art, and drama. By writing metaphorically or allegorically, a poet can provide a complex of meanings, enabling the reader to experience a wide variety of imagery while reading the poetry. Denotative symbols, on the other hand, are the language of science, practical affairs, and everyday discourse.

A metaphorical symbol may also encompass opposing ideas. By calling her lover the sun, a woman may wish to convey in addition to the conceptions mentioned before the feeling that he is not faithful to her since he periodically disappears from sight leaving her in darkness, or that he is remote and unapproachable, or that he is too hot-blooded. Symbols that express conflicting ideas or feelings are filled with dramatic tension. That is another reason why poets and dramatists are so fond of using them.

Let us elaborate on the distinction between the two kinds of symbols, denotative and metaphorical. Here is a simple example. The words *dog* and *cat* in the sentence, "The dog chased the cat," stand for two kinds of animals. One can point to them or draw a picture of them. They are purely denotative word symbols without any surplus meaning. But if one says of a person, "He is a dog," or "She is a cat," it is clear that the words are being used metaphorically and not denotatively. By using the name of an animal, the speaker intends to express a particular attitude about the person. What this attitude is depends upon the speaker's conception of the animal. If he conceives of a dog as a lowly, brutish creature, then the person he calls a dog is regarded by him as having these qualities. The expression "son of a bitch," conveys this pejorative attitude in even stronger language, since the insult implicates the person's mother. When a woman is called a cat or catty, it is clearly intended to be uncomplimentary. Pussy, however, carries a sexual connotation, as does the term "cat house." Kitten, on the other hand, implies cuteness. To call a man a fox means he is sly and cunning. Wolf has become a standard expression for a sexual predator, chicken for a coward, hawk for a warlike person, and dove for a peace-loving person, owl for a wise individual, and goat for a victim, as in scapegoat.

The referent of a denotative symbol is something that can ordinarily be pointed at; the referent of a metaphorical symbol cannot be pointed at because it is a subjective mental attitude or feeling. The distincion is shown in the following diagram.

DENOTATIVE SYMBOL	REFERENT
The word *fox*	The animal *fox*
METAPHORICAL SYMBOL	REFERENT
The idea of a person	The idea of a fox
as being crafty (foxy)	as being crafty

The relation of a denotative symbol to its referent is usually arbitrary. A fox could be called by any other name, and is in other languages. The relation of a metaphorical symbol to its referent is not arbitrary. It may be poetic or prosaic, but there has to be an identity between the idea of the symbol and the idea of the referent. A person's conception of someone whom he calls a fox agrees with his conception of the animal. Misunderstandings may arise among people when their ideas of the referent object differ.

Metaphor is often objected to as being too subjective and personal for precise and accurate communication. Instead of calling him a fox, why not just say that he is sly and cunning? Expressed in that way, there would be no misunderstanding. Others feel that conversation and literature would be pretty dull without the use of metaphor. Slang, which is almost entirely metaphorical, is regarded by many as being a picturesque form of expression because it forms interesting pictures (images) in the mind. By others, slang is considered to be a coarse and crude way of expressing oneself.

Most dream images can be regarded as literal denotations of referent objects and events. If a person dreams of fighting, eating, or having sexual relations, these can be treated as being purely denotative and do not require decoding. They are exactly what they say they are and have no surplus meaning. Some dream images are metaphorical and do have surplus meaning.

How can metaphorical images in dreams be identified? There is no precise answer. No one has discovered an infallible rule or method for differentiating denotative and metaphorical symbols in dreams. To say that this or that element in a dream is metaphorical is only a conjecture or a hypothesis that has to be confirmed by other evidence. Let us discuss some of the methods that have been used.

Nocturnal Emissions

We have found that dreams which culminate in an emission, although no sexual acts or feelings appear in the dream, often point to interesting metaphorical representations of sexual activity. Consider the following dream which was reported by a young unmarried man.

> I dreamed I got out of bed and went to the bathroom and attempted to turn on a water faucet. I turned and turned but no water came. I then decided to call a plumber. Soon afterwards the door opened and an individual dressed in coveralls approached me. Upon closer examination I discovered the plumber was a female. I scoffed at the idea of a lady plumber. But, unruffled, she went to the basin, turned the faucet, and water immediately flowed. This was when the emission occurred.

There is nothing overtly sexual in this dream, yet the fact that it culminated in an orgasm indicates some of the elements of the dream are metaphorical symbols for sexual referents. Faucet may be construed as a symbol for the dreamer's penis, the turning of the faucet as genital manipulation, and the flow of water as the ejaculation.

This type of decoding is only a first step. It is not very interesting psychologically to learn that a faucet can stand for a penis. What is of significant interest is the dreamer's way of symbolizing sexual gratification. The choice of metaphors reveals what he thinks about sex. In this faucet dream it is clearly a plumbing conception. Sexual fulfillment is obtained by a mechanical discharge of liquid through a pipe. His idea of a suitable sexual partner is expressed by the image of a masculinized woman, clothed in coveralls, who performs her function quickly and mechanically. She merely turns the faucet-penis and water-seminal fluid flows.

A dreamer is usually not so limited in his conception of a particular activity that he uses the same symbol over and over again. A few nights later, the same man dreamed that he was lying in bed in the early morning.

It was a cold, dull morning and I seemed to feel a chill run through my body. Suddenly the sun rose and the room filled with warmth. It was then the emission occurred.

In this dream, the young man chose a metaphor from nature to convey his conception of sex. Sexual feeling is like a warm sun. As the sun rises, the dreamer's sexuality also rises. The room (his body) is filled with the sun's warmth, and he ejaculates.

This young man had another sex dream a few months later in which there was no metaphorical symbolization.

I tried to seduce a young woman only to find that my organ seemed to be too large for her vagina, thus making intercourse impossible.

No decoding of this dream is necessary. Penis is penis, and vagina is vagina. It is a straightforward representation of a sexual relation although, it is to be noted not a very satisfactory one since it did not result in an orgasm.

The unsatisfactory nature of this open sex dream suggests another reason why metaphorical symbols appear in dreams. In the metaphorical dream of the faucet, the young man imagined how much better it would be if his penis worked as easily as operating a faucet. No sooner was this imagined than his penis was transformed into a faucet. The dreamer was not aware of the transformation, but his body nevertheless acted appropriately by producing an ejaculation.

We happen to know from other sources that the young man whose dreams we have been discussing had never experienced sexual relations with a woman, and was sexually frustrated. In order to achieve sexual gratification he chose to create a whole new set of conditions in his dreams, including a better-functioning penis. When he dreamed about his penis as it actually was, he failed to gain satisfaction.

This type of dream, as we have said, is valuable for elucidating metaphorical symbols. When a man has a "wet dream" in which he removes a large cap from a fire hydrant and water gushes out like a geyser, the phallic nature of the fireplug is not likely to be missed by anyone. Most "wet dreams" are not metaphorical, however. They usually occur when a person is dreaming about having explicit sexual relations. Nor does the turning on of a faucet, a rising sun filling a room with warmth, or a gushing fire hydrant necessarily refer to sex in other dreams where they appear.

Bladder symbolism can also sometimes be detected in dreams. For example, a man dreamed that the tire on his bicycle ruptured. This was followed by the image of water running in an alley. Finally, the dreamer stepped into a bathroom to urinate.

It was observed that the dreams of mental patients contained fewer metaphorical symbols as their condition worsened and more such symbols as their condition improved. For instance, a young woman in an early stage of schizophrenia dreamed of a cow getting stuck in the mud. In a later stage of her psychosis, she dreamed of pushing her mother into a pile of manure. Both dreams presumably mean the same thing, namely, hostility toward the mother, but the former one is metaphorical and the latter one is denotative. In the first dream, cow stands for mother and mud symbolizes manure. In the second dream, mother is mother and manure is manure.

Free Association

The method of free association was employed by Freud for the purpose of discovering the meaning of dreams report-

ed by patients undergoing psychoanalysis. As used in psychoanalysis, every element in a dream is free-associated to, even
though not every element is necessarily symbolic.

Here is an example of how the free-association method
works. A young unmarried woman who was undergoing
treatment for anxiety attacks related the following dream.

> An elephant was chasing me. I ran home but the door was
> locked and I couldn't get in.

Her associations to the first sentence were as follows.
"I'm afraid of elephants. Their long snakelike trunks and
little mean eyes terrify me. My father took me to a circus
when I was little. There were lots of elephants. They climbed
on each other's back. They waved their long trunks in the air
and made loud trumpeting noises. I was scared and I cuddled
close to my father. His breath smelled bad and his eyes were
half-closed and bloodshot. I guess he was drunk. He often
was. I cried and wanted to go home. My father was a great
big man. He had dark gray hair and a long red nose. I used
to be afraid of him."

To the second sentence she gave the following associations.
"I guess I was running home to my mother. She used to
protect me from my father when I was a child. When I
became older, she didn't seem to care about me anymore.
She didn't care about anything except her little dog, Snooky.
She shut us all out of her life."

From these associations, the dreamer arrived at the
following interpretation of the meaning of the dream. "The
elephant is my father who is chasing me. I run to my mother
for protection but she locked me out."

Probing by the therapist revealed additional information
about the dreamer's feelings toward her father. Once she had
seen her father naked and she had been fascinated and
appalled by the size of his sex organs. Sometimes her mother
locked the door when her father was out late. He would
pound and pound and make such a racket that she finally let
him in. The patient cowered in bed and held her breath until
her mother opened the door. Then she would become excited
and strain her ears to hear what they were saying. Her father
would shout at her mother and call her names. Then they
would go to bed and the patient would lie awake wondering
what they were doing. Once she got up and tried to get into
her parents' bedroom but the door was locked. She heard
heavy breathing and creaking bedsprings.

On the basis of this additional information, the dream was given a further interpretation. "I wanted to sleep with my father like my mother did but I was afraid he might hurt me. If my mother had locked us both out of the house then we could have gone away together. I would have my father all to myself."

In this example, we see how a dream is used as a springboard to elicit information from a patient. Much of the information had little to do with the dream itself. Once the dreamer associated elephant with her father and home with her mother, the symbolic significance of the dream was clarified. The psychoanalyst then proceeded to learn more about the patient's attitudes toward her mother and father, information he could have obtained without the dream.

The free-association method can also be used to decode a single element in a dream which is thought to be symbolic. Here is an example. A young man who was employed in a service station dreamed one night that he was checking the oil level in a car driven by an attractive young woman. One of the images in the dream consisted of seeing himself insert the dipstick in the oil reservoir. When he was asked to free-associate to this element, he replied that it reminded him of inserting his penis into a vagina. For this dreamer, as for the young man who had the faucet dream, sex is conceived of as purely mechanical activity.

We used the method of free association to determine who the male stranger represents in dreams. According to Freudian theory, the stranger stands for the father. In order to test this hypothesis, free associations were obtained from a group of young men and women to each mention of a male stranger in their dreams. An analysis of the associations revealed that in more than half of them some reference was made to the dreamer's father or another authority figure, such as army officer, priest, grandfather, step-father, or another person's father. Rarely did the associations implicate the mother or any other female. These results confirmed the hypothesis that the stranger in dreams often stands for the dreamer's father who is supposed to be the first stranger the child encounters.

An interesting sidelight of this study was that some of the associations referred to the dreamer himself. He saw himself as the stranger, that is, someone estranged from the world.

Amplification

Carl Jung developed another method for deciphering symbols in dreams. This is the method of amplification. Amplification differs from free association in the following respects. In free-associating to a dream element, a person gives a linear set of verbal responses. The first association leads to a second which leads to a third and so on until the line ends. Amplification requires the person to concentrate on a dream element and to produce a set of responses which are directly related to that element. The result is a constellation of associations around the dream element instead of a line of associations that may lead far afield from the original element.

In the free-association method, the dreamer alone produces the associations. In the method of amplification, the analyst as well as the patient may contribute material. Ancient writings, mythologies, religious texts, fairy tales, and other sources may be consulted to provide additional information about the dream element.

Here is an example in which the analyst performed all of the amplification. The patient dreamed:

> I was fishing for a trout, not in an ordinary stream or lake but in a reservoir divided into compartments. For a time I fished with the usual equipment of flies, etc., but I caught nothing. Becoming exasperated, I took up a three-pronged spear, which was lying nearby, and immediately I succeeded in spearing a fine fish.

The element to be amplified was the three-pronged spear. The trident is the main attribute of the Greek god, Poseidon (Neptune in Roman mythology). Poseidon has many qualities and roles. He is the god of the sea and co-equal with Zeus and Hades in ruling the Cosmos. He is also the god of earthquakes, which he produces by driving his trident into the earth. Poseidon creates as well as destroys. Every time he uses his trident something creative happens, a spring wells out of the earth or a valley opens between the hills. As the analyst noted, "Besides this, Poseidon is the god of storms. He also is a stormy lover, has affairs with all sorts of creatures producing many offspring, so that he is creative also in this sense. He is the god of the earth and as such is responsible for fertility, in particular plant fertility; he is in that respect called the farmer. Then he is a horseman *par excellence* and has created the first horse by using his trident. Then he is called the father of men." Poseidon was also a Delphic oracle, a doctor, and the father of two famous doctors. In short, Poseidon is a creative god, and the trident is his creative tool.

This dream initiated a healing process in the patient which led to his complete recovery from a serious depression of three years' standing. The trident symbolized the creative powers within the patient which had remained inhibited for so long.

One difficulty in using the method of amplification, a difficulty that is also encountered in using the free-association method, is how to go from the great mass of material that is often produced back to the dream element, and to decode it correctly. How does one select from the various amplifications or associations the one that applies to a specific element in a specific dream?

The following example illustrates this difficulty. A person had three dreams in which a turtle appeared. When asked to amplify turtle, he produced seventeen pages of associations. Turtles meant among many other things: amphibiousness, independence, oral aggressiveness (biting), slow but sure, ugliness, restriction of freedom, and primitiveness.

When we look at the dreams, we see that the turtles in them have little connection with the consciously contrived amplifications. In the first dream, the man is trying to lift a little turtle out of a bowl. It slips out of his hand a number of times but he finally obtains a firm grip on it and removes it from the bowl. In the second dream, he and a group of men are watching a medium-sized prehistoric turtle crawl across the ground. They discuss its place in evolution, and the dreamer maintains, against opposition, that the turtle is closely related to the bird. In a third dream, he is looking at a very large prehistoric turtle in a pool of water. It is biting something. The dreamer is discussing wtih a companion when biting appeared in evolution. He imagines that many different animals are just now beginning to bite all over the world. Only two items in the list given above bear a relation to his dreams, the turtle as a biting animal and prehistoric.

Dream Series

The dream series method enables one to amplify an element that appears in a number of dreams without asking the dreamer for his associations to it. One can determine what significance the element has for the dreamer by observing what role it plays in each of the dreams in which this particular element is mentioned.

Here is an example. From a dream diary kept by a middle-aged man, we selected twenty-five dreams in which the dreamer was involved with a body of water. In eleven of these dreams, the dreamer or another person was in danger of drowning, or had a mishap in the water. In nine dreams, the dreamer was threatened by sharks or other underwater animals. In one dream, a friend had built a device to kill skindivers. The dreamer was pleasantly swimming in four dreams.

The dreamer's prevailing conceptions of water was that it is a dangerous place; one is likely to drown or be attacked by sharks. The following dream portrays this conception.

(The boat they are on is damaged.) It is necessary for us to get into the water. We are worried that the whole thing is going to sink, leaving us to drown. There is fear every time we go into the water because the ocean is likely to be full of sharks and other dangerous animals. With every stroke in the water there is fear of hitting or being struck by one. We know now death is imminent, but there is no panic, just quiet despair, really, in fact, resignation and acceptance of death. It's sad but pretty in a way. Now that we've fought well and done all we could to survive, death seems almost a reward, a relief for tired contestants being taken out of the game.

Note also in this dream the strong expression of a wish for death.

We made an analysis of the role of stairs in the dreams of a woman. In twelve dreams, the dreamer had a mishap or was threathened by something while going up or down stairs. In eight dreams about stairs, she had a sexual experience. All but one of these experiences occurred while she was going upstairs. This corroborates the idea that ascending stairs has a sexual connotation. In several dreams, she was going upstairs to get a better view (voyeurism?). In some dreams, stairs played a neutral or indifferent role.

An advantage of the dream series method is that meanings of dream elements are revealed by the various contexts in which they are used in the dreams, and not by material that lies outside of the dreams.

Dream Sets

The meaning of an object or activity in dreams can also be determined by analyzing sets of dreams. This type of analysis tells us what a particular dream element means for a group of people.

For example, an analysis of 35 dreams of swimming that occurred in a set of 1000 dreams obtained from young adults showed the following conceptions. The most prevalent one (as in the individual dreamer discussed in the preceding section) was fear of being attacked or having a mishap or drowning. The second most prevalent one referred to the sexual aspects of swimming. Several women dreamed they had intercourse with a man under water, and several others dreamed of their bathing suits coming off while in swimming with a boyfriend. One dream seemed to point rather clearly to swimming as representing a return to the womb. It may be significant that women dreamed three times more often about swimming than men did.

We also analyzed the dreams in which rings appeared. In women's dreams there was often something wrong with an engagement ring. They also dreamed that their ring was being admired by a man or it was being stolen by a man. As a counterpart to this last theme, men sometimes dream of stealing diamond rings.

Hypnosis

Dream symbolism has also been deciphered by means of hypnosis. It is suggested to a person while he is under hypnosis that he will have a dream in which a referent is to be represented by a metaphor. The type of metaphor to be used is not suggested to him. Here are a few examples.

A hypnotized man was told he would have a dream of sexual intercourse. He reported the following dream.

This fellow and girl go horseback riding. They're taking it easy, just riding along. Then, the girl decides to race her horse. He races his. They race for a mile. Both horses are foaming. The fellow and the girl are laughing.

Another hypnotized man was told to dream about masturbation. He dreamed as follows.

This fellow's taking an exam. It's a very hard exam. He gets tense. As he looks at the paper he gets more tense. His face gets flushed and his hand begins to shake. He knocks the paper and pencil off the desk and drops his head on the desk from exhaustion.

Another procedure is to take an element from an actual dream and ask a hypnotized person to decipher it. Some people are able to do this. An eighteen-year-old girl was given the following instructions after she had been hypnotized. "Dreams have meaning. Now that you are asleep (hypnotized) you will be better able to understand them. A girl dreamed that she was packing her trunk when a big snake crawled into it. She was terrified and ran out of the room. What do you think the dream means?" The hypnotized girl replied, "Well, I guess she was afraid of being seduced. The snake would be the man's sex organ and the trunk hers."
Several hypnotized individuals were given this dream to interpret.

A boy was sitting at his desk studying when the wastebasket caught on fire. He ran and got a pitcher of water and put the fire out.

Their responses were "He wet the bed" or "He should have gone to the bathroom."

Although the belief that the sleeping mind expresses ideas and feelings in metaphorical images is a very old one, no one, to our knowledge, has actually observed a referent change into a symbol or a symbol change into a referent *within the dream itself*. Such an observation would prove without question that there are metaphorical symbols in dreams.
It was our good fortune to acquire a dream (the only one out of 50,000) in which a symbol was transformed into its referent during the course of the dream. The dreamer was a psychologist who was tape-recording his dreams for us.
In the first part of the dream, a group of humanoid aliens who had been visiting Earth were preparing to depart in their

spaceship. (The dreamer is a science fiction fan and often has science fiction dreams.) The dreamer was bidding farewell to one of the humanoid girls.

> I started going into the open port of the spaceship, where the girl was, in order to say good-bye. The dream changed such that going into this port I was sticking my penis into her vagina from a rear entry position. This surprised me in the dream, the sudden change, and apparently surprised the girl, too, both of us quite pleasantly. She rolled over into the conventional position and yet somehow she was still the spaceship in a way. Her rolling over so we could get into a normal front entry position upset everything in the spaceship. It turned people over and rolled loose objects around. Also my penis inside her vagina sort of symbolically, well actually, pushed around objects in the spaceship somehow.

Entering a spaceship (the symbol) is transformed into sexual penetration (the referent). Note the way in which the dreamer describes this transformation. "The dream changed such that going into this port I was sticking my penis into her vagina." He does not say that the scene changed from entering a port to having intercourse; rather, the image of entering a port and the image of putting his penis into her vagina occurred simultaneously. The referent existed side by side with the symbol. This same juxtaposition of referent and symbol is seen when he says, "yet somehow she was still the spaceship in a way." The girl was not *like* a spaceship; she *was* the spaceship. Observe also what he says in the last sentence. "My penis inside her vagina sort of *symbolically, well actually,* pushed around objects inside the spaceship somehow." At first, speaking like a sophisticated psychologist who is too astonished to report what he experiences, says that his penis must be "sort of symbolically" pushing objects around in the spaceship. He then acknowledges that what he *actually* experienced in the dream *was* pushing objects around in the spaceship with his penis.

We see in this dream the concomitant appearance of at least three symbols and their referents: spaceship and girl, port and vagina, and entering a spaceship and entering her vagina with his penis.

The presence of metaphorical symbols in dreams seems to be fairly well established. The larger question of how to decide which dream elements are to be considered metaphorical and not merely denotative has not been and probably cannot be answered. We can only list here some of the criteria we have found useful in making such a determination.

One important criterion is the appearance of a bizarre or unusual image in a dream. A horse that talks, bullets that have no penetrability, bloodstains on the lining of a white purse, wearing old shoes to a wedding, running naked in the streets, teeth that crumble in the mouth, a bridge that collapses, a piano whose keys are stuck together, a woman who carries a plumber's snake to a party—all suggest that the dream images are metaphorical rather than denotative.

Another useful criterion is the appearance of something that seems to be illogical in a dream. A young man dreamed that his girlfriend pulled a pistol out of *his* pocket and begged him to shoot her. He was embarrassed but she pleaded with him until he obliged her. Then he laughed. This dream makes more sense if the gun is considered to be a metaphorical symbol for the young man's sex organ.

A third criterion is the repetition of an uncommon element in a series of dreams. A person, for example, dreamed repeatedly of holes. By treating holes as metaphorical symbols it enabled us to draw some interesting conclusions about the dreamer's problems.

We regard all animals as being metaphorical unless they belong to the dreamer or his family.

Finally, when we feel our understanding of the dream can be expanded by treating dream elements as metaphors, we do not hesitate to do so. One of our students was interested in exploring the unconscious feelings of young men and women about the genitals. She assumed that certain objects in dreams represented the sex organs. Symbols for the penis consisted of elongated objects capable of penetration, including such things as guns, knives, poles, pencils, airplanes, and keys. Symbols for the vagina consisted of hollow objects and enclosures capable of being entered, including such things as caves, shoes, rings, and rooms.

Then she read a large number of young adult dreams and noted what qualities these "phallic" and "vaginal" objects possessed. She found, for instance, that sometimes they were impaired or defective. The dreamer had a broken pen or a tarnished ring. Sometimes the sexual symbol was used aggressively or it aroused fear. Sometimes it fulfilled the dreamer's desire to possess the symbolic object.

The most frequently expressed attitudes about phallic symbols in male dreams were impairment and aggressiveness, and in female dreams were wish for and fear of phallic symbols.

The two most common attitudes about vaginal symbols in male dreams were dislike and fear of, in female dreams impairment and rejection.

The results of this interesting study substantiated, to some extent, Freud's theory that men worry about loss or impairment of the genitals and women want what they do not have. A number of other attitudes about the genitals were also expressed. Women are often afraid of the penis as well as wanting to possess it. Men also fear the male organ, and like women they wish they had a better one. Women sometimes value the vagina; men almost never do.

This study does not prove that there *are* symbols in dreams. It does show that by assuming there are symbols in dreams one can learn a great deal about deep-lying feelings and attitudes.

One thing we frown upon is the use of dream books, be they popular or "scientific," for translating symbols into their referents. By merely decoding symbols in such a mechanical fashion, little or nothing is gained for better understanding the dreamer.

The use of dream books is based on the assumption that there are universal metaphorical symbols in dreams. We are dubious about the truth of this assumption. When we examined ancient dream books, very few of the dream elements listed in them occur in modern dreams. People today are dreaming about different things than they were a thousand years ago.

We do believe there are *conceptual equivalents* among dream symbols. That is, two different elements like a spear and a gun may both be phallic symbols. When spears were used, people dreamed about spears, and when guns replaced spears, guns appeared in dreams. The spear and the gun represent an aggressive conception of the male organ. That is why we call them *conceptual equivalents*. A gun and a banana may also both symbolize the penis, but they are not conceptual equivalents because they express different conceptions of the penis.

A useful dream book would be one in which conceptual equivalents (synonyms) for the same referents would be brought together. The making of such a dream book is not feasible yet, because we do not have enough information about what people dream in various parts of the world.

We would like to make two final comments on symbols in dreams. First, as we have said before, dreams can be analyzed without resorting to symbolic interpretations. Content analysis alone can provide a great deal of information about the dreamer without probing for symbolic meanings.

Secondly, it bears repeating, that the translation of symbols into referents is only a first step. It is of far greater significance to determine what the use of a particular symbol tells us about the dreamer's conception of the referent. Riding a horse, entering a cave, climbing a ladder, plowing a field, and inserting a key into a lock may all represent sexual intercourse, but the conceptions conveyed by these images are quite different.

As we shall try to demonstrate in Chapter 7, metaphorical symbols in dreams have their exact counterparts in waking life. That is, if a gun represents an aggressive sex symbol in a dream, it also represents the same conception in everyday life.

Chapter 5

Consistencies
in Dream Series

When a person begins to keep a record of his dreams, he will not, at first, recognize any connection of subject matter from one night to the next. The dreams will appear completely dissociated from each other, occurring in a random fashion.

As the number of dreams in the record increases, then the dreamer will begin to recognize repetitions, regularities, and consistencies. The same characters, situations, activities, and objects, and the same themes repeat themselves. There will appear to be lots of variation when dream samples are selected at random, but when the entire dream record is considered, the elements tend to follow a pretty well-defined pattern.

In this chapter we will present evidence to show how much consistency there is in long dream series, and then we will offer an explanation of why this consistency exists in an individual's dreams. First, let us distinguish three types of consistency.

The first type we call *absolute constancy*. Suppose we have a dream diary that has been kept for ten years and we conduct a content analysis of the dreams year by year. If the frequency with which a given element appears continues to remain the same year after year, this is what is meant by

absolute constancy. There will always be slight random variations, but these are of no significance.

Here is an example of this type of consistency. The proportion of characters who were males and the proportion
who were females in six hundred successive dreams of a
middle-aged man over a seventeen-year period were as follows:

DREAM SETS

	1-100	101-200	201-300	301-400	401-500	501-600
Proportion of males	.63	.61	.57	.63	.62	.60
Proportion of females	.37	.39	.43	.37	.38	.40

There are slight variations in the proportions of male and
female characters but they are not significant variations.
(Statistical tests of consistency can be employed but we will
not go into these technicalities here.)

A second type of consistency is *relative consistency*. If we
make a comparison between any two elements, relative consistency exists when the incidence of one element exceeds the
incidence of the other element. In the foregoing example, the
proportion of males is greater than the proportion of females
in every set of dreams.

One may compare more than two elements to determine
their relative consistency. For example, four objects that
frequently appeared in the dreams of this middle-aged man
were body parts, furniture, clothing, and printed matter. In
his six hundred dreams, the incidence of body parts always
exceeded the incidence of furniture, furniture always exceeded clothing, and clothing always exceeded printed matter. In
other words, the rank order of these four classes of objects
remained exactly the same throughout seventeen years of
dreaming.

Finally, there is *developmental regularity*. Here there is a
change from one period of time to the next, but it is a
consistent change. The frequencies (or proportions) either
become larger or smaller. For example, the middle-aged
dreamer had an increasing number of aggressive interactions
with family members over the seventeen-year period covered by the dream diary. They jumped from a fairly low
proportion of .17 during the early years to an exceedingly
high proportion of .68 in the latter years. Most of this

increase was due to an increasing number of aggressions and hostilities with his wife.

These three types of consistency are found whenever a long dream series is analyzed. Developmental regularities are much less common than relative consistencies. There is a considerable amount of absolute constancy, but not as much as relative consistency. We have analyzed more than a score of long dream series, and have never found an exception to this generalization. The dreams of an individual are amazingly consistent in subject matter from one year to the next. After analyzing the first several hundred dreams in a series, the process becomes rather tedious due to the repetitious nature of the dream content.

The longest dream series we have spans the years between early adulthood and old age. This half-century of dream reporting began in 1912 when the dreamer, whom we shall call Dorothea, was 25 years old, and terminated a few days before her death in 1965. Dorothea was born in China where her parents were American missionaries. She was the second of eight children. The family returned to live in the United States when Dorothea was 13 years old. She was awarded a doctorate in psychology in 1925, and taught in colleges and universities until poor health forced her to retire. She continued to be active in her profession, and published a number of articles after her retirement. Dorothea was never married.

We took 600 of her dreams and divided them into sets of 100. The first set covered the early adult years; the last set consisted of dreams recorded when she was 75 years old. Each set was scored for characters, aggressions, friendliness, and misfortunes. These are the results of the analysis.

The proportions of single characters, plural characters, and animals in Dorothea's dreams did not change over the fifty years, nor did the proportions of family members, friends and acquaintances, and strangers. There was a tendency for more females and fewer males to appear in her dreams as she grew older, which probably reflected a change in her life situation. In later years she lived in a retirement home for women, and had fewer contacts with men.

She dreamed about her parents and siblings with the same consistency throughout the fifty years, although her father died when she was very young and her mother died when Dorothea was 61. The number of aggressive and friendly interactions Dorothea had with various classes of characters did not change appreciably throughout the years. Nor did the number of misfortunes.

Ten themes which occurred with considerable frequency in Dorothea's dreams were identified. The frequencies of six of these themes remained pretty much the same throughout the whole series. They were:

1. Food and eating dreams; one out of every five dreams was of this type,
2. Loss of an object belonging to the dreamer, which occurred in every sixth dream on the average,
3. Appearance of the dreamer's mother in every tenth dream,
4. Dreamer is in a disorderly or small room, or her room is being invaded by others in every tenth dream,
5. Dreamer going to the toilet in every twelfth dream,
6. Dreamer late or concerned about being late or missing a bus or train in every sixteenth dream.

There was some sort of consistent change in three of the themes. She dreamed more about being ill in the earlier years than in the later years. This corresponded with the actual situation. Dorothea was more troubled by illness when she was younger. She dreamed more about traveling when she was a young woman, when she actually did a lot of traveling. Not surprisingly, she had more dreams of babies when she was younger.

One theme showed an increase in frequency followed by a decrease. This was the theme of being left out, not waited on, or ignored. As a young active adult, this had not been a problem. During her middle years it did become a problem because she was unmarried and also because, being a woman, her professional advancement had not been as rapid as she deserved. As she grew old she became more reconciled to being ignored.

We made a special study of regression in Dorothea's dreams. By regression is meant dreaming about an earlier period of one's life. One may dream of a house in which he lived as a child, of a childhood friend, of a person who has been dead for years, or of an activity he engaged in years ago. It is believed old people live more in the past than younger people do. Dorothea's dreams gave us an opportunity to test the validity of this belief. When we scored the dreams for regressive elements, we found to our surprise that there were just as many "remembrances of things past" in her dreams when she was twenty as there were when she was seventy. She dreamed about her past with the same frequency throughout her life. This is another indication of the consistency one finds in dreams.

Another woman, Marie, kept a record of her dreams when she was in her twenties and again when she was in her sixties. Virtually all of the frequencies were the same in the two sets of dreams. There were the same number of males and females, and the same kinds of objects. There was the same proportion of friendly and aggressive interactions with each class of character. There was even the same number of prominent persons and Negroes in the two sets of dreams. There was an amazing amount of consistency despite a forty-year difference in age.

Several differences were noted, however. When Marie was in her sixties, she was dreaming about more strangers than when she was in her twenties. This may have been due to the fact that her husband and all of her relatives had died (Marie had no children), and that many of her close friends were no longer living near her. She lived alone in a small town several thousand miles away from where she was born and raised.

In her twenties, Marie had dreamed more often of being the victim of aggression, especially from males, whereas in her sixties she was more often the aggressor. Marie felt this change was due to more self-confidence and assertiveness.

The number of sex dreams fell off markedly when Marie was in her sixties. During the earlier years she had been fairly promiscuous, and later in life, due to an operation, she had no sexual outlets whatsoever. In this case, dreams did not compensate for what she lacked in waking life. The impulse had apparently vanished in reality as well as from her dreams.

In this connection, we have another series of dreams that covers a number of years. This man recorded 100 dreams when he was 38 years old. Twenty-four of the 100 dreams were sexual. When he was in his early sixties, he recorded another 100 dreams, of which 33 were sexual. This shows that the sex drive as expressed in dreams need not abate with age. Nor could the larger number of sex dreams at the later age be considered compensatory. He was, in fact, having more sexual outlets at age 60 than he was at 38. The dreams reflected the actual state of affairs in his life.

In her dreams, Marie used many color names to describe various objects and settings. The same frequencies were found for the different colors in the two sets of dreams with one exception. In her earlier dreams she rarely described anything as being black; in her later dreams there were many references to black. This change may be due, Marie believes, to the association of black with mourning and death.

Another one of our dream correspondents, whom we shall call Jeffrey, kept a record of his dreams between the ages of 37 and 62. During this twenty-five-year period, the various elements in his dreams—objects, characters, and interactions—remained highly consistent. There was a slight tendency for the number of immediate family members to appear less frequently and for strangers to appear more frequently as he aged. This may have been due to the fact that Jeffrey left his home and family when he was fifty and thereafter was exposed to more contact with strangers. This trend began to appear in his dreams, however, before he separated from his family, which suggests that the alienation had begun before the actual separation took place. This is confirmed by a steadily increasing number of aggressive interactions with family members over the years.

An interesting series was obtained from a young man, Jasper, who kept a dream diary between the ages of 15 and 19, the years of adolescence when so many changes in behavior and personality are presumed to occur. Jasper was an eccentric person in waking life. He suffered from a variety of phobias and obsessions. which resulted in a breakdown requiring hospitalization and psychiatric treatment. One might expect to find a considerable amount of inconsistency or change in the dream content throughout the five-year period. His dreams did show slightly more variation than the other dream series we analyzed, but, in general, consistency prevailed.

There were some important changes, however. At age 15, Jasper dreamed more about people known to him, and at 19 he dreamed more often of strangers. This increase was due entirely to more male strangers of his own age appearing in his dreams. The number of friendly interactions with strangers also increased from a low level at age 15 to a high level at 19. From other information we learned that Jasper's friends during early adolescence had turned against him because of his eccentricities, and he was looking for new and better companions among strangers. In reality, he actually did succeed in acquiring new friends.

The number of sex dreams increased from zero at age 15 to a very high number when he was 19. This developmental change is not surprising. The high frequency at 19, which was much higher than the average young man of this age, was accompanied in waking life by a complete lack of gratification aside from frequent masturbation.

Dorothea, Marie, Jeffrey, and Jasper kept dream diaries out of curiosity. The next person, Raymond, recorded his dreams by request of his therapist. He kept a record of his dreams for the 20 months he was undergoing psychotherapy at an outpatient clinic. An analysis of the dream contents showed little or no change during these 20 months. He was dreaming about the same things with the same frequency at the termination of treatment as he was at the beginning.

One change was observed which might have indicated some improvement. The proportions of family members and strangers decreased, and the proportion of known persons increased during the period of treatment. This could signify that he was moving away from dependence upon his family and from feelings of alienation toward closer relationships with his peers.

We do not have in our possession a dream series that extends from childhood to adulthood. Unfortunately, children do not keep dream diaries. What we did, however, was to compare the dreams of children with the dreams of adults. When this was done, a number of differences appeared. As already noted, children dream about animals to a far greater extent than adults do. This helps to account for the greater amount of aggression in children's dreams, since aggression with animals is high at any age. It also helps to explain the more frequent occurrence of physical aggression in children's dreams since violence is the rule when the aggression is with an animal. Children suffer more misfortunes in their dreams than adults do, but at any age there is much more misfortune than good fortune. Children rarely have sex dreams.

Children experience only slightly more anxiety in their dreams than adults do, and the kinds of situations that cause the dreamer to feel anxious are the same for children and adults. There are some differences in the frequency with which the various types of anxiety dreams occur. Anxiety in the child's dream is more frequently caused by being chased or attacked by animals and monsters. In adult dreams, the dreamer himself often produces the anxiety by committing some crime or socially disapproved act. The adult dreamer may use a more indirect approach to produce anxiety. He imagines some adversity that causes illness or harm to him or one of his possessions.

It is interesting that there was no difference between children and adults in their attempts to cope with the threatening situation. Children tried as often as adults did, which was not very often, and they were equally successful when they did try to overcome the threat. Success at any age is quite uncommon, however.

In general, then, the dreams of children appear to be somewhat more primitive than the dreams of adults as indicated by the larger number of animals, more violence, and the greater frequency of chase and attack dreams. On the other hand, children do not experience overt sex dreams, which in adults are often expressed in quite primitive ways.

Let us now consider some of the explanations that might account for the great amount of consistency in the subject matter of dreams over long periods of time. A favorite explanation for the consistency of an individual's dream life is that a person lives in a fairly constant environment. He does the same things, sees the same people and surroundings, year in and year out. Dreams do not change because the person's environment does not change.

The validity of this explanation is seriously challenged by the following considerations. None of the individuals whose dream series we have analyzed and discussed in this chapter lived in a stable environment. Between the ages of 25 and 75 Dorothea's life changed in fairly drastic ways. She held a number of positions in various parts of the United States, traveled widely throughout the world, suffered disabling illnesses at various times, lost her mother and some of her siblings, and moved from her own dwelling into a retirement home. The same was true of Marie's life. In the forty years that elapsed between the two periods of her dream records, Marie had married and lost her husband, moved from one coast to the other, changed vocations, and engaged in new activities and hobbies.

Nor can it be said of Jeffrey that his environment during the twenty-five years of dream recording had remained more or less constant. He lived in a number of places in the United States and Europe under a variety of conditions and circumstances. He held different positions that entailed different responsibilities and working conditions. He separated from his wife. Old friends were no longer seen and new ones were made. His father and brother died; his daughter, who was a child at the beginning of the dream diary, had married by the end of that period. Jasper, the eccentric adolescent, and Raymond, the epileptic, did not live in stable environments either.

When we take a closer look at the dreams of Jeffrey and
Marie, the truth of the old adage "things change but everything remains the same" is exemplified. In Jeffrey's case, we
compared 344 dreams he recorded during one five-year period with 308 dreams he recorded during another five-year
period 13 years later. Our reason for selecting these periods
is that drastic changes occurred in Jeffrey's life between
them. During the first period, he was living with his wife and
daughter in a large city and was teaching school. During the
second period, he lived alone and did not teach. He lived in
Florida for three years and then in California for two years.
During these five years he traveled widely in the United
States and in foreign countries. We were interested to see
whether the characters in his dreams changed between these
two five-year periods, and whether the types of interactions
underwent any significant changes.

First, we made a list of the characters in both sets of
dreams whom Jeffrey knew by name. There were 127 such
characters in the first set of dreams, and 94 in the second set.
Only 17 persons appeared in both sets. Of these 17, six were
family members: mother, father, oldest brother, middle
brother, wife, and daughter. These six persons constituted the
entire family of the dreamer. Of the remaining eleven, two
were individuals with whom the dreamer had a continuing
relationship over both periods. Nine persons who appeared in
both sets of dreams were those whom the dreamer had
known either during the first period or at some earlier time
in his life.

In general, then, the cast of characters was quite different
in the two sets of dreams. Who were these characters? Aside
from family members, they were individuals whom Jeffrey
associated with at the time he dreamed about them. When he
was recording his dreams in City A, where he lived during
the first period, he dreamed about people whom he saw quite
frequently in that city. When he moved to City B, they were
replaced by the new friends he made in that city, and when
he moved to City C, the cast changed again. Occasionally, a
person out of his past would enter a dream, but this was the
exception rather than the rule.

It was interesting to watch the changes in the cast take
place when Jeffrey moved from one place to another. For a
while after relocating he continued to dream about his
former friends and acquaintances. Then gradually people from
his new circle of friends began to appear in his dreams. After

a few months in the new location, the transformation was virtually complete. The frequency with which he dreamed about various people in each of these locations was an accurate measure of the intensity of the relationship with them.

Despite the change in the cast of characters, the proportions of characters who were males and females remained the same, and the proportions of aggressive and friendly interactions with them also remained the same. What this means is that the elements (persons) in a system of human relationships can change completely without altering the nature of the system. For example, female A in the first set of dreams was replaced by female B in the second set, and male A was replaced by male B, but the way in which Jeffrey interacted in his dreams during the second period with female B and male B was the same way he had interacted with female A and male A in his dreams during the first period.

It is plausible to explain this finding in terms of a stable personality pattern within the dreamer which determines the identical relationships he will form with people in each new setting. The person's behavior in his dreams remains the same despite a change in environment because he remains the same person.

The "eternal ones" of dreams are the dreamer's immediate family. They continue to appear long after the dreamer has left home and even long after they have died. There is something about the nature of these relationships that causes them to continue indefinitely. At least, this is true in dreams, and we suspect it is true in waking life as well.

Jeffrey's dreams about his wife, from whom he separated between the first and second set of dreams, are especially interesting. She was the most frequently appearing character in both sets of dreams, appearing in 72 dreams of the first set and 33 dreams of the second set. No other character approached these frequencies.

Jeffrey's dreams about his wife were primarily aggressive. During the first period he had 23 dreams in which an aggressive interaction took place, and only three dreams in which friendliness was expressed toward his wife. The number of aggressive interactions continued to mount until the marriage was dissolved.

What happened then? He still continued to dream about his wife, and he still continued to have predominantly hostile dreams. According to the dreamer's subjective appraisal of his feelings about his wife in waking life, they were ambivalent (as virtually all close relationships are) and weighted on the positive side. Their separation was an amicable one and they have maintained friendly relations since. The dreams tell a different story. There was an abundance of hostile feelings in the dreamer which physical separation did not diminish.

Why should he continue to dream about his wife while he ceased to dream about his best friends after separation took place? The answer lies partly in the fact that a best friend in one location can be replaced by a best friend in the new location. Friendship is transferable. Apparently, no one can replace one's wife because of the complexities of the relationship. Even when a person remarries, his first wife still appears frequently in his dreams.

We have observed in other dream series that a wife will dream about her husband for years after his death. One of our informants had two husbands and she dreamed about both of them throughout the rest of her life.

The relationship of a man to his wife has many parallels with his relationship to his mother. And it will be recalled the dreamer's mother appears in his dreams throughout his life. Some evidence for the equivalence of wife and mother is found in Jeffrey's dreams. Following his separation from his wife, he dreamed more often of his mother who had died many years before. All of Jeffrey's interactions with her in these dreams were aggressive ones. Moreover, he was sometimes unable to tell whether it was his wife or his mother in a dream.

We also made an analysis of the animals that appeared in Jeffrey's two sets of dreams. From 1946 to 1950, he dreamed about 12 different species of animals, and from 1963 to 1967, he also dreamed about 12 species. Five of the species were the same in both sets, and they accounted for 75 percent of all the animals appearing in each set of dreams. The dog was by far the most popular animal followed by fish and snake (tied for second place), cat, and rat. There was only one known animal common to the two sets of dreams. This was a dog that belonged to the dreamer until 1959.

Jeffrey's interactions with and feelings about the animals in his dreams were classified under three headings: neutral, negative, and positive. There was almost exactly the same proportion of each feeling in both sets of dreams: neutral .36 versus .33, negative .58 and .54, and positive .06 and .13. All of the positive interactions were with dogs. All of the other animals appeared in either neutral or negative roles.

Here again we see not only a high degree of consistency but also the fact that the characters can change without affecting the types of interactions the dreamer has with them.

An analysis similar to the one made of Jeffrey's dreams was performed on Marie's two sets of dreams which were separated by an interval of 40 years. Of the 71 characters whose names she knew in the early dreams, and the 103 characters whose names she knew in the later dreams, only 14 were common to both lists. Five of these characters were the dreamer's mother, father, aunt who was her guardian after her parents died, and two relatives. Four of the characters were individuals with whom the dreamer continued correspondence over the years. The other five she had no contact with for forty years. These results are very similar to those obtained from an analysis of Jeffrey's dreams.

An interesting fact emerged when we compared the number of known male and female characters in Marie's two sets of dreams. The number of *different* male characters remained the same, but the number of *different* female characters known to the dreamer doubled. However, when we compared the total number of *appearances* that each male and female made in Marie's two sets of dreams, we found that the ratio of males to females did not change over the forty years. This means that although there were fewer males relative to the number of females in the second set, the fewer males appeared more often so that the sex ratio remained the same.

We found the same thing in Jeffrey's dreams. Fewer characters in a class are compensated for by more frequent appearances of each character. The child molester rarely dreamed of any known women, but he dreamed repeatedly of his mother and sister. These observations suggest that a person has just so much energy which can be used for maintaining his social relations. If he expends most of his energy on one or two persons he will not have much left for others. He can have a lot of friendships of little intensity by spreading the energy thinly, or he can have few friendships of great intensity by concentrating the energy.

The majority of known characters in Marie's two sets of dreams (except for members of her family and her husband) were people with whom she was in contact, and the frequency of their appearance was related to the intensity of feeling Marie had for them. During her twenties, the most frequent person in her dreams was her aunt who raised her after Marie was orphaned. In her sixties, Marie's deceased husband was the most popular character, leading the second-place aunt (who was also dead) by a large margin. Just as Jeffrey dreamed more about his mother as he grew older, so Marie dreamed more about her father as she grew older.

Although the cast of characters in Marie's two sets of dreams was altogether different, with a few exceptions, the proportion of aggressive and friendly interactions with males and females remained almost identical. The cast changed but the play remained the same.

We observed in an earlier chapter that one's dreams like one's experiences in waking life consists of the dreamer's interactions with people and animals and his interactions with objects. We have just seen that interactions with dream characters are much the same from one year to the next, and even when the characters change, the dreamer's interactions with the new characters are almost the same as they were with the old characters. Does the same consistency prevail with respect to his interactions with objects? The answer is, yes, it does.

Let us examine some of the evidence upon which this affirmative answer is based. In order to make such an analysis, objects have been selected which recur with sufficient frequency in order to provide substantial evidence.

In every dream series we have analyzed, there is a constant recurrence of certain objects and activities, and the dreamer's involvement with these objects and activities remains much the same throughout. We have already had occasion to refer to some of these consistencies. Holes and shafts appeared with considerable regularity throughout the 1400 dreams reported by the child molester, and his reactions to them did not vary. He always conceived of them as something to get out of or into. Decrepit houses were a recurring feature of Tony's dreams, and there was no change in his perception of them. For Tony, decaying houses were deplorable and dangerous, and he had a desire to renovate them. The surfer dreamed with unvarying regularity of surfing activities, mostly of watching the waves and other surfers. Automobiles played the same role in Jeffrey's dreams for twenty-five years.

One might explain this by saying that the constancy of the environment in dreams merely reflects the constancy of the environment in waking life. In a sense, this is true. Houses, automobiles, food, windows, trees, money, and clothes are common objects in dreams and waking life. It should not surprise us to learn that a dreamer who is an avid tennis player often dreams of his favorite pastime, or that a man who dresses in women's clothes in his dreams does the same when awake. One naturally dreams about a world of objects and activities with which he is familiar. What else is there to dream about?

This explanation does not really solve anything, however. One does not look into a mirror expecting to find out who he is. Reflection is not explanation or understanding. We ought to ask, as we shall later, why a person's daytime environment as well as his nocturnal one remains constant. We believe that the prevalence of familiar objects in dreams and the ways in which the dreamer interacts with them illuminates the psychological significance of these objects.

At this time, we would like to focus on another problem with respect to environmental constancy. We have noticed in analyzing long dream series that a person will repeatedly dream of an object which is *not* a part of his present environment, or an activity in which he no longer engages. Karl dreamed repeatedly of his childhood home, which he rarely visited, of football, which he no longer played or watched, and of submarines, which were hardly a part of his Midwest surroundings. All of these things were firmly embedded in his memory; they were as much a part of his consciousness as the objects and activities of his current life were. Perhaps even more so. His boyhood home, football, and submarines lived on in his dreams because they were associated with wishes and fears that were still active in him. They probably will continue to haunt his dreams and his waking thoughts as long as he lives. The irony of this situation is revealed in a dream in which he sees himself dead and buried in a football stadium. Even in death he cannot bury memories of football.

In discussing the consistency with which people appeared in dreams we observed that the people changed when the dreamer acquired a new set of friends, but the dreamer's interactions with them remained much the same. Does the same thing happen with respect to objects and activities? It is obvious that it does. When a person moves to a new city, the surroundings there gradually take the place of the old locale in his dreams. How he interacts with this new environment duplicates the interactions with his old environment. This should not surprise us since it happens in waking life as well. How a person drives a car is not going to change physically when he changes cars.

More interesting is the replacement in dreams of one set of

elements by a completely different set. The clearest example of this is the way in which animals are replaced by physical objects and activities as a child grows older. Dangerous lions, tigers, and alligators transform into dangerous trucks, trains, and machinery. The replacement is never complete, however, because many animals still appear in adult dreams and play the same threatening, aggressive roles they do in children's dreams. Obviously, the automobile has virtually replaced the horse in dreams during the last hundred years. Recall how the port of a spaceship replaced the female genitals in the science fiction dream.

What is the explanation for consistencies in the contents of dreams? We rejected the idea that constancies in the dreamer's environment produce consistencies in his dreams because we have shown that dreams remain consistent despite environmental changes.

We prefer the hypothesis that constancies in the personality account for consistencies in dreams. We believe the person is a fairly stabilized organization of personality traits, attitudes, and behavioral patterns. He is, as the saying goes, a creature of habit. No matter where he goes, these habits of thinking, feeling, and acting go with him. They even follow him into the world of sleep, so that he is the same person awake or asleep.

What is the origin of this stabilized personality? Three answers have been suggested. The first answer attributes it to heredity. Stable patterns of behavior are inborn. This answer may be correct but it is virtually impossible to prove. The science of genetics has devised methods for showing how physical features are controlled by the genes, but no methods have been developed for showing how the genes may determine patterns of dreaming, thinking, feeling, and acting, except for some fairly simple patterns of animal behavior and some pathological conditions in man.

Jung posited that the mind of man is filled with archaic material deposited early in racial history but, of course, he was unable to demonstrate a relationship between germplasm and these archetypes. Nor did he try. He felt there must be a genetic basis for mental life because the mind, like the body, has features that are universally distributed and recur in every generation. This is an attractive theory for which Jung and his followers have supplied a lot of indirect evidence. In an impressive study, Jung demonstrated a high degree of congruence between the dreams of a man living in twentieth-century Zurich with the rituals, symbolism, and practices of fourteenth-century alchemists.

When we were in Zurich we related a dream to a group of Jungian psychologists. The dream was about a dog pulling on the dreamer's arm. The dreamer had been suffering for some days with acute bursitis in his shoulder, and when he awoke from the dream the pain had disappeared and never returned. The Jungians were serious in their belief that the dog of Asclepius, who often cured patients at the ancient temple of Epidaurus for his master, was the dog of the dream who cured the dreamer. To Jungians, the dog was an archetypal figure.

A study of animals in dreams offers some data that can be interpreted in line with Jung's archetypal theory. At the age of four, 61 percent of children's dreams contain animals. Thereafter, the percentage of animal dreams declines until age 18, when it stabilizes at about 7 percent.

Since four-year-olds have not had much experience with animals, and since the incidence of animals in dreams decreases as experience accumulates, it is not implausible that the high percentage during early years is due to memories laid down in the collective unconscious when man lived much closer to animals. Moreover, these animal dreams are filled with aggression and terror. "A bear was chasing me." "A crocodile ate me up." "I killed a big snake." Dreams of this nature suggest a primitive origin, when men and animals preyed upon each other.

Another explanation for these findings may occur to the reader. It may be that children dream about animals because many of the stories they are read at bedtime are about animals. It is true that dreams of animals and stories about animals have much in common. The Jungian might reply that the interest children have in stories about animals is itself a manifestation of an animal archetype.

Another finding of animal dream research is that primitive adults have more animal dreams than civilized adults do, and the more primitive the group, the higher the incidence of animal dreams. This result would support Jung's idea that the collective unconscious remains more influential in people whose mind has not been so overlaid by education and culture as to conceal the archetypes.

The second answer is that consistency within the individual is due to a set of experiences he has during fetal development which condition him to react in habitual ways. This theory is also difficult to verify. We cannot plant a memory in the fetus and wait for it to appear in a dream years later.

In one study we tried to reconstruct the type of experiences that the unborn organism is likely to have in the womb, and then see if any of these experiences appear in dreams.

What is the fetal environment like? It is a life of confinement and restraint, increasing more so every day as the fetus grows larger. It is a life of changing pressures as the mother moves about performing various physical activities. The womb is a world of darkness and restriction. The fetus can experience sounds, however, that penetrate from the external world. Also the mother's body and the fetus itself produce sounds, but most of these sounds are experienced as vibrations rather than audible noises. One constant stimulus for the fetus is the vibration of the mother's heartbeat. It was observed that playing a tape recording of a beating heart provided a soothing effect on babies. This finding agrees with the observation that both monkey and human mothers have a marked preference for holding the baby on the left side (heart side) irrespective of whether the mother is right- or left-handed.

Since the fetus is suspended in a fluid-filled container (the womb) within a larger container (the mother's body), movements of the fetus tend to be synchronized with those of the mother. Consequently, a variety of movements are experienced by the fetus. The fetus makes movements, too, which are self-stimulating.

The first step in gathering data was to formulate definite criteria for identifying representations of the fetal environment in dreams. These consisted of such items as the dreamer being in a room, automobile, ship, cave, water, forest, or any other type of enclosure or confined space; being restrained, confined, or crushed; experiencing up and down motion; being in a thick fog or darkness; gasping for air; being in a slimy or wet place; not being able to see or hear; and feeling warm and secure.

Two other types of representations were also analyzed: being born and its opposite, returning to the womb. Being born can be expressed by leaving or trying to leave any type of enclosure, getting out of bed, falling out of a car, and being freed from restraint. Returning to the womb is symbolized by entering any type of enclosure, getting in bed, being submerged, being eaten, and seeking protection.

Then 590 dreams were analyzed, and in 370 of them, one or more of the foregoing items were found. Two-thirds of all the representations were of the fetal environment, and there were also more birth symbols than symbols of returning to the womb.

Here are some examples. A young man dreamed he was flying an airplane through a heavy rainstorm.

The plane became flooded and my breathing became heavier. Shortly I could breathe no longer and I began to gasp for air.

This dream contains a reference to the fetal environment, flying (movement) in an airplane (womb), and a representation of birth, flooding of the airplane (breaking of the membrane), and gasping for air (as the newborn baby does).

Another young man represented the fetal environment by a flying dream.

It seemed as if everything around me was moving very smoothly—velvety smooth—when all of a sudden the moving through space became very rough.

In this dream, the dreamer's ambivalence toward life in the womb is suggested by smooth and rough flying, which corresponds to the gentle and abrupt movements of the mother's body.

The following portrayal of an idyllic prenatal existence was found in a dream reported by a young woman.

Last night I was sailing in a sailboat which was really a big wooden shoe. The night was warm and beautiful, and lovely music floated through the air. I was in a very blissful state. I grew sleepy. I heard Brahm's *Lullaby* and it was too much for me. I fell into a deep sleep.

In the next dream, life in the womb has two aspects, one of being crushed, the other of sinking into blissful depths.

I was walking down the street and had the feeling of being crushed in the masses of humanity. I had to escape so I began to run. I came to a lake where there was a small boat. Across the lake was utopia. I started to row and about halfway across the boat sunk.

The womb is represented in the next dream as a boiler, and birth as a violent ejection.

I was working inside a large boiler with several other men and there was a slight escapage of gases through the pipes of the boiler. They were in weak concentration and therefore did not affect us, but they were highly explosive. Someone lighted a match and no sooner had this been done than everyone rushed toward the opening of the boiler. We all escaped but the blast of the gases threw everyone hurtling through space.

This study does not prove irrefutably that fetal memories appear in dreams, but the evidence, circumstantial though it may be, points in that direction.

The third answer ascribes constancy of behavior to a set of childhood experiences whose influence persists throughout life. This explanation has been most fully elaborated by Freud. Freud believed that our behavior is determined mainly by impulses (wishes) of which we are not conscious. These impulses or wishes have either never been conscious or they have been repressed in early childhood because they produce anxiety. These unconscious impulses strive for expression but they are blocked by repression. They try to find substitute outlets which avoid anxiety, but the substitutes do not entirely satisfy the wishes despite continuous attempts.

Some of the wishes and their attendant fears that emerge in childhood and persist throughout life are: the child's desire for the mother and fear of rejection or separation; desires for the breast and other oral gratification and fears of deprivation; wishes and fears surrounding toilet training; curbs on pleasurable body stimulation, such as stroking of the genitals; competition with brothers and sisters for the mother's affection; and, above all, the celebrated Oedipus complex—love for the mother and fear of the father. An infinite number of variations are played of these few basic themes throughout life.

These conflicts between wishes and fears are timeless and imperishable. Freud flatly declared, "The contents of the unconscious are not altered by the passage of time."

Why do these few basic themes persist throughout life? Because they can never be concluded; they remain forever unfinished and unfinishable. Fear sees to that. Consequently, the basic motivations of our behavior, both awake and in dreams, are the same at age sixty as they were at six. There are endless variations in persons, objects, and activities, but the game remains the same.

Dorothea's dreams provide an excellent example of conflicts between a few basic wishes and fears endlessly acted out.

One of her most frequent dreams was about food and eating. It occurred in every fifth dream. There was no systematic change in the incidence of this theme over a half-century of dream reporting. The topic is obviously orality, which was first experienced during infancy when the pleasure of being fed by mother and the terror of sudden deprivation of food and mother were embedded in Dorothea's mind.

In many of her oral dreams, Dorothea is not given food although others at the table have plenty, or the food is removed from her plate before she has a chance to eat. As a child in a large family (she was the second of eight children), Dorothea had ample opportunity to experience feelings of being ignored, or of being displaced by a newcomer. Another motive for this dream is guilt and self-punishment. She is deprived of food in her dreams when she does or thinks of doing something wrong.

Children often conceive of eating as a form of cannibalism. The baby at the breast fantasies it is eating its mother. The punishment for these body-destruction fantasies is to be deprived of the breast. This is supposedly the baby's conception of weaning.

Dorothea dreamed about her mother every tenth dream even though her mother had been dead for many years. This also suggests the tenacious hold the dependency period can have upon the mind of an adult.

The bathroom theme was also a recurring feature of Dorothea's dreams. Often she is interrupted by someone entering the bathroom. This is reminiscent of the toilet-training period. The infant's private pleasures of relieving himself whenever he desires become a public frustration of schedules, threats, and blandishments when training commences. The wish is to return to the time of spontaneous elimination; the fear is that she will be caught and punished for indulging in a sensual pleasure.

Related to this bathroom theme is the recurrent dream in which Dorothea feels concerned about missing a bus, train, or ship. This anxiety about being on time has its counterpart in "being on time" in getting to the bathroom. It is conjectured that all schedules originate from this first schedule that is laid out for the child. The theme of being late is also related to separation anxiety, the child's fear of being abandoned by the mother.

Losing or mislaying an object, which is often Dorothea's, purse, was another prevalent dream subject. There was no increase in the incidence of this dream during the fifty-year period, which proves it is not related to the forgetfulness of older persons. An object that contains something, as a purse or handbag does, is said to symbolize the female reproductive system. When one dreams of losing a purse, one is being punished for something, perhaps sexual fantasies. The loss may also represent a wish to lose one's femaleness. Loss of a phallic-shaped object like a pen or a gun or a fishing pole is said to represent castration.

The girl's feeling of being incomplete because she lacks the visible genitals of the male gives her a negative attitude toward her own body. This attitude is not helped any by the process of menstruation, a period regarded by people everywhere as a time when the woman is unclean. This feeling expresses itself throughout Dorothea's dream diary by frequently dreaming of being in a room that is messy and disorderly. Sometimes the room is small, which signifies the restrictions of life. In other dreams, the room is entered by people, which annoys Dorothea. Like the bathroom dream, this suggests that her privacy (that is, her private pleasures) is being invaded as it was when she was a child. It may not be a coincidence that "privates" or "private parts" are expressions for the genitals.

The idea that dreams are motivated by wishes and fears experienced in childhood is especially attractive because it is able to account for the subject matter of so many dreams.

Before concluding this chapter, we would like to emphasize another point which supports the view that one's dream life is fairly constant. For at least a hundred years, scientists have been trying to influence the subject matter of dreams by a variety of experimental procedures. Two of the most commonly used procedures are (1) to stimulate a person just before he goes to sleep, and (2) to stimulate him while he is asleep without awakening him. One form of presleep stimulus that has been used is to show a person a movie, then see whether any elements of the movie appear in his dreams. A variety of stimuli including sounds, verbal material, pressures on the body, touching the skin with warm and cold objects, dropping water on the person, and tilting or vibrating the bed have been applied to the sleeping person to see whether it influences his dreams.

Presleep experiences and stimulation during sleep do influence dreams in observable ways but the magnitude of the effect is usually insignificant. Elements of a movie, or a noise or a pressure, may be incorporated in a dream without changing the basic theme of the dream. Nor is there any evidence that external stimulation can cause or initiate a dream.

Internal bodily conditions, however, may influence the subject matter of dreams substantially, or even produce a dream. Bladder tension may be accompanied by a dream of a person relieving himself. Hunger may result in a dream of eating, or sexual tension in a sex dream. Even in these cases, the dream may not reflect the bodily state exactly. Or the bodily state may be incorporated into an ongoing dream which has a different basic theme.

Constancies in dream life cannot be overemphasized, although a few changes do take place. Jeffrey had an increasing number of aggressive interactions with members of his family. More male strangers entered Jasper's dreams. Raymond dreamed about an increasing number of friends and acquaintances. Dorothea had fewer dreams of babies as she grew older.

One of the most amazing changes we know of took place in the dreams of a patient undergoing treatment for an emotional disorder. When he began treatment, his dreams consisted entirely of inanimate objects. No person, animal, or vegetation occurred in them. As therapy progressed, plants began to appear, followed by insects and other lower forms of life. Gradually, his dreams worked their way up the phylogenetic scale until finally he was dreaming about people. As his dreams changed, his waking behavior also changed. This case is probably quite unusual.

What causes dreams to change in a systematic manner is a difficult question to answer. Psychotherapy or psychoanalysis may initiate changes. Or an upsurge or an abatement of a particular impulse with age may alter some aspects of one's dream life. The number of sex dreams shows a marked increase during adolescence. Changes in the body or radical changes in the environment may sometimes alter the subject matter of dreams. The menstrual cycle in women is accompanied by consistent changes in their dreams. For example, they become more active socially and aggressively, especially with males, just prior to or during menstruation. Dream content changes during the later stages of pregnancy. Themes of being physically and sexually unattractive, and apprehension that husbands might find other women more attractive, are quite common in the dreams of pregnant women. There are also many anxiety dreams of giving birth to a malformed baby.

The fact that dreams are resistant to change and remain

quite constant in their subject matter over long periods of time suggests to us that when a developmental regularity does occur it indicates some important change is happening in the life or personality or physical condition of the dreamer which may merit attention. It could be symptomatic of something serious which can be treated or dealt with before it has progressed too far. For example, a change took place in the dreams of a man who was sending us his dreams every week. The change consisted of an increasing number of bizarre dreams and nightmares. We felt this reflected something pathological and urged him to see a psychotherapist, which he did.

Chapter **6**

Dreams
and Waking Behavior

What is the nature of the relationship between dreams and waking behavior? When we consider only the bizarre dreams that people have, we might think there was no relationship at all. How often one exclaims when awakening from an absurd dream, "What nonsense! How could I ever dream that?" Most dreams are not nonsensical or bizarre, however.

Some scientists believe there is an inverse relationship between what we do in our dreams and what we do in waking life. Our unfulfilled wishes in waking life are fulfilled or an attempt is made to fulfill them in our dreams (Freud). Or a part of our personality that has been neglected in waking life finds expression in dreams. That is, dreams play a compensatory role (Jung). Others believe that conflicts and tensions which disturb us during the day are resolved during the night. An ancient belief was that dreams are the opposite of what will occur in waking life. To dream of good fortune signifies that the dreamer will have bad luck.

There is a good deal to say in favor of this view of an inverse relationship between dreams and waking behavior. We have found numerous examples where a person who is sexually frustrated in waking life has many sex dreams. Or a person who suppresses his aggression during the day has wildly aggressive dreams during the night. It is an attractive notion but we do not find it to be true.

A large number of dreams reflect rather faithfully the daytime activities and preoccupations of the dreamer. Skiers dream of skiing, surfers dream of surfing, and mountain climbers dream of climbing mountains. Teachers dream of classroom situations, bankers dream of banking activities, and nurses dream about their patients. Alcoholics dream of drinking, child molesters dream of molesting children, and arsonists dream of setting fires. Husbands dream about their wives and wives dream about their husbands, children dream about their parents and parents dream about their children, and good friends and lovers dream about each other.

These facts and many others obtained from the content analysis of many dream series have led us to formulate what we call the *continuity hypothesis*. This hypothesis states that dreams are continuous with waking life; the world of dreaming and the world of waking are one. The dream world is neither discontinuous nor inverse in its relationship to the conscious world. We remain the same person, the same personality with the same characteristics, and the same basic beliefs and convictions whether awake or asleep. The wishes and fears that determine our actions and thoughts in everyday life also determine what we will dream about.

How can we reconcile the continuity hypothesis with the obvious fact that a person will do something in his dreams that he would not or could not do in a waking state? He will, for example, torture someone to death, have sex with his young daughter, betray his best friend, or fly through the air.

The answer to this dilemma is to be found in the distinction between overt behavior ("acting out") and covert behavior (thoughts, feelings, and fantasies). The continuity may be between dreams and covert behavior or it may be between dreams and overt behavior. A person who has many sex or aggression dreams may either have many fantasies of sex or aggression when he is awake, or he may have many actual sexual or aggressive experiences. In either case he is preoccupied with sex or aggression, awake or asleep. Although when asleep these preoccupations have fewer limitations, which allows the dreamer to experience tremendous diversity in his sexual and aggressive fantasies.

It is interesting that the discontinuities between acting out in waking life and acting out in dreams pertain almost exclusively to the impulses of sex and aggression, although discontinuities are sometimes found in other situations. A woman who often dreamed of traveling in foreign countries had never left the United States. She had many fantasies of visiting other countries, had read much about them, and had many foreign friends. Adolescent girls dream of getting married and bearing children before there is much chance of this happening, but, of course, they often daydream about it, too.

We do not dream about everything we do in waking life. Usually we dream only about that which is important to us in a very personal way. Preoccupations rather than occupations are more likely to form our dreams. There are trivial and prosaic dreams, but they are not the ones we are likely to recall.

As we will point out in the next chapter, symbolism in dreams parallels symbolism in everyday life. Fetal environments in dreams—ships, caves, rooms, passageways, tunnels, water—are also fetal environments in waking life. Phallic symbols—trees, guns, pens, poles, automobiles, airplanes— are phallic symbols awake or asleep. There is no discontinuity with respect to symbolism.

Dreams often open our eyes to our true feelings, which we close our eyes to when awake. We were astonished to find in the dreams of the Mount Everest climbers so many negative feelings about climbing. Failure, misfortune, resentment, and a desire to get the whole expedition over with and return home plagued their dreams. Here are a few examples.

We failed miserably on the mountain so we went back to the village.

The four men who were in the summit area were blown off the mountain by Communist Chinese jets.

I was back home. I had come home early. I couldn't see why we had failed but we had. We were tired of living up there.

I was climbing with a man up the West Ridge. I looked back and saw a child fall off the cliff. The child's father was the man I was climbing with.

Speaking of the Mount Everest climbers, we attempted to evaluate their interpersonal relations from a content analysis of their dreams. The study was a failure. For example, we said of two climbers whose dreams we had analyzed that they were very likely the most popular members of the team, that they were admired for their skills, vitality, maturity, high morale, and dependability, and that they were looked up to as leaders of the expedition. We could not have been more wrong. These two men were regarded by their teammates as immature, undependable, self-centered, and generally obnoxious. They were the most unpopular members of the expedition.

Why was there this great discrepancy between what we saw in their dreams and what their fellow climbers saw in the two men. One possibility is that the personal characteristics we found expressed in their dreams were inappropriate in the setting of an arduous physical undertaking that required careful planning and attention to detail. The dreams of these two men were filled with an open, exuberant display of warm and vital human impulses. There were almost no manifestations of anxiety, guilt, sadism, or other pathological symptoms that so often appeared in the dreams of the other climbers. They were the dreams of psychologically healthy individuals who found pleasure in living. Such a person is bound to be a thorn in the flesh of those who are repressed, defensive, anxious, sober, and overcontrolled.

This taught us not to make predictions from dreams of how a person will be judged by his associates in a group situation, unless we know something about the requirements and demands imposed by the situation and the makeup of the group. A happy-go-lucky person may be the life of the party but a disaster on a grueling mountain climb. By the same token, we do not make judgments about people appearing in a person's dreams. How he sees them in his dreams may not be the way they are in reality.

In our investigations of the relationship between the contents of dreams and waking life behavior, we have used several methods. One method consists of doing a content analysis of dreams recorded by famous or well-known people and comparing the results with material about the dreamer obtained from biographies and autobiographies. We used this method in two studies, one of the dreams of Freud and Jung, the other of the dreams of Franz Kafka. Since both of these studies have been published, we will limit our discussion of them here to the highlights.

In the Freud-Jung study, there were many similarities in what these two famous psychologists dreamed about, but there were also striking differences.

Jung reported his dreams at greater length than Freud did. This agrees with their respective writing styles. Freud's writing is generally regarded as being terse and compact, Jung's as being discursive and prolix.

More people came into Freud's dreams than into Jung's. This agrees with observations of the sociability of the two men in waking life. Freud was a sociable person who had many close friends and disciples. Jung was more solitary. He liked to be by himself, and even built a retreat where he could be alone with books and nature. Jung's social life centered around his family, and his dreams reflected this fact by containing many family members.

The two men had about the same amount of friendliness in their dreams, but Jung always initiated the friendliness, whereas in Freud's dreams the friendliness was nearly always initiated by another person. It is said that Freud expected people to come to him. On one occasion, his feelings were hurt because Jung did not make an effort to visit him when Freud was in Switzerland.

There were many more references to food and eating in Freud's dreams than in Jung's. Freud smoked an enormous number of cigars, which supposedly contributed to the development of cancer in the mouth. Freud dreaded being dependent upon anyone. An intense fear, as Freud himself pointed out, usually hides a wish for the very thing of which one is afraid. Freud's dread of being dependent was, according to this Freudian hypothesis, a reaction against an unconscious wish to be taken care of. This wish develops during the oral stage when the baby is dependent upon the mother. Freud's high incidence of oral dreams reflected an infantile wish behind an adult fear.

The most interesting difference between the dreams of the two men was in the aggressive-friendliness pattern with male and female characters. The typical male dreamer has more aggressive interactions with male characters, and more friendly interactions with female characters. Jung's pattern conformed fairly close to type. Freud's pattern was the reverse of the typical one; he had more aggression with females and more friendliness with males. Many people have inferred from his writings that Frued was hostile toward women. Ernest Jones, his friend, fellow psychoanalyst, and biographer, said Freud's attitude toward women was "old fashioned." He considered the main function of women "to be ministering angels to the needs and comforts of men." Women were enigmatic for Freud. "What do they want?" he asked his friend Marie Bonaparte. Jones said Freud was attracted to masculine women. He was also "quite peculiarly monogamous." "The more passionate side of married life subsided with him earlier than it does with many men," Jones informs us.

Freud had several intense friendships with men. He spoke of overcoming his homosexuality, and admitted that alternations of love and hate affected his relationships with men. Jones speaks of Freud's "mental bisexuality." Freud once wrote to a colleague, "The affection of a group of courageous and understanding young men is the most precious gift that psychoanalysis has bestowed upon me."

It appears, then, both from his dreams and from his own testimony and that of his biographer that Freud had an inverted Oedipus complex, which colored his dreams and his personality. There is no evidence from Jung's life that he had anything other than the typical male Oedipus complex.

Another prominent person, Franz Kafka, the celebrated author of *The Trial* and *The Castle,* recorded 37 of his dreams in his diaries and letters. We analyzed these dreams and found seven major themes:

1. *Preoccupation with the body.* This concern is evidenced by the high incidence of references to body parts in Kafka's dreams.

2. *Body disfigurement.* Disfigured bodies occur fairly frequently in Kafka's dreams.

3. *Emphasis on clothing and nakedness.* References to clothing and to nakedness exceed those of the comparison group.

4. *Looking* (*scoptophilia*). This theme is represented by looking and witnessing and by reaction formations against looking, such as blindness.

5. *Passivity.* Kafka's passivity in his dreams is indicated by a low incidence of aggression, sex, personal success, and activities.

6. *Ambivalence toward men and women.* Kafka displayed the same incidence of aggression and friendliness with males and with females. This is an atypical pattern for male dreamers.

7. *The masculinized woman.* In some dreams, Kafka described a female character as being masculine in appearance or dress. This rarely occurs in male dreams.

We then went to Kafka's diaries and letters and to biographies to see whether these seven themes were evident in his waking behavior. They all were. He was very concerned about his body, worried continuously about his physical health, compared his body to the bodies of other men to his own disadvantage, was interested in nudism and nature cures, and had doubts about his sexual capacity. "Every imperfection of the body tormented him," his intimate friend and biographer, Max Brod, wrote.

Kafka was excessively interested in clothes, and his diaries are filled with descriptions of what people were wearing. He himself was always well dressed. With regard to the looking theme, Kafka acknowledged that he was an "Eye-man."

Kafka was a passive person in waking life as well as in his dreams. Brod reported he was entirely lacking in push. Kafka characterized himself as being weak, timid, hesitant, and lacking in confidence. There are many references in his diaries to resting and sleeping or not being able to sleep. He never married and lived most of his life with his parents. His physical activities were noncompetitive, and there is no evidence that he was physically aggressive.

Kafka was ambivalent toward men, especially his father whom he loved and hated, admired and feared. He was also ambivalent toward women. He had off-again, on-again affairs with several women. Twice he was engaged and twice he broke his engagement to the same woman.

The masculinized women of his dreams were represented in waking life by his mother, who was masculine. She was a strong, stalwart person who went to work with her husband and played cards with him at night. Kafka saw his parents as conspirators against him.

Another method we have used to investigate the relationship between dreams and waking behavior, is to ask the dreamer to supply us with information about himself *after* we have analyzed his dreams and before we know anything about him other than his age and sex. Specific questions are asked the dreamer, and we predict what his answers will be. We can then determine the percentage of correct predictions.

In one study, our inferences about the dreamer were checked by a psychologist who had counseled the dreamer and knew a great deal about his life and personality. This was a study of a child molester.

From his dreams, we inferred that he was polymorphously perverse, meaning that his sex drive expressed itself with a variety of sexual partners—males and females, children and adults, and animals—and employed a variety of sexual contacts—normal intercourse, active and passive anal intercourse and fellatio, and masturbation. There was also a lot of voyeurism in his dreams. He had engaged in all of these sexual outlets and practices in waking life.

We inferred from the high frequency with which his mother and sister entered his dreams, and from the low frequency of known males and females in his dreams, that he was closely tied to his family and had few friends. This inference was correct.

From the high incidence of minors in his dreams and many friendly and sexual interactions with them, we inferred that he himself had not grown up. There was a lot of evidence from his waking life to corroborate this.

One of the most unusual features of his dreams was the attribution of male characteristics to females, and female characteristics to males. In his dreams, women had penises, beards, and were disguised as men. The dreamer dressed in women's clothes, thought he would make "a magnificent woman," was told he had feminine charms, and had a chest that protruded like a woman's breast. This confusion of gender found in his dreams is reflected in waking life by statements that he has always been baffled by what it means to be a male and a female. "When I masturbate I am both male and female."

There was an enormous amount of urinating and defecating in his dreams, from which we inferred he was unable to control his impulses. Although he is not incontinent as an adult, he often was as a child. And, of course, he has difficulty controlling his sexual impulses, for which he has been arrested a number of times.

He also tended to have both in dreams and in waking life a closer identification with women than with men, a preference for a protected, fetal-like environment, and an undeveloped conscience.

Tony, a man in his middle thirties, kept a record of his dreams for a year and sent them to us to be analyzed. Since there were many references in his dreams to teaching school, we assumed he was a schoolteacher (which was correct), and since there were no references to a wife, that he was unmarried (which was also correct). The strategy we used in this study, as in other studies of individual dream series, was to make predictions of Tony's behavior, attitudes, and feelings from frequencies that either exceeded or fell below the norms, and from a qualitative analysis of his dreams. Tony was then asked questions about his behavior without knowing what we had predicted. Our predictions were then compared with his answers. The following 32 predictions were confirmed by the answers he gave.

1. He is not an aggressive person. Tony had fewer aggressive interactions in his dreams than the average man does.

2. He is not ambitious or competitive. There were few attempts to achieve something in his dreams.

3. He has felt increasingly more alienated from people during the past year. The number of strangers in his dreams increased during the time he was sending us his dreams.

4. He is afraid of being on high places. There were dreams of falling or fear of falling such as the following one.

> I am perched dangerously on top of a swaying brick column. Loose material was falling. I was trying to decide if I dare descend safely. A boy near me plunged down and hit with a thud, presumably dead.

5. He is afraid of being in confined places. He had a number of dreams in which he was in a narrow cave or confined in an underground room.

6. He is concerned about growing old. There were dreams about physical incapacities and aging. He dreamed of losing his hair and of it turning gray. He was the person referred to in an earlier chapter who identified himself with crumbling houses. In writing to us on this subject, Tony said: "I have often thought how great it would be to be an adolescent again. For many years I have placed an extremely high premium on youthful charm and beauty. The slow deterioration of age bothers me." This answer also helps to explain his associations with adolescents which are referred to below.

7. He is fairly conscious of time. There were many references to time in his dreams. Tony said that he was a very punctual person. "I try to see that no one has to wait for me and I expect that from other people."

8. He is careful with money. There were many references in his dreams to money and financial transactions of the following sort.

> I got my statement from the savings association. I tried and tried to decipher and discover the balance. Finally I asked a woman. She said I had none. It seems they had withdrawn $52.00 from my account. She wanted me to draw a circle around the figure. I had just put in $19.52 or $19.29 in coins that I should have had in my account.

He admitted that he could pinch pennies pretty tightly.

9. He does not feel particularly secure and comfortable in his house. We made this prediction because there were so many dreams of old, dilapidated houses and dreams in which unwanted and disturbing strangers were living in his house, such as the following ones.

I had bought another house. There was much work to be done. I had to turn off the water because of a leak. There was a dirt floor. One wall was made of lathe-like strips. The window panes needed replacing.

I suddenly discovered to my amazement a number of people had moved into my third floor. I learned they had no place to go, but I was adamant about their leaving my house.

10. He wet the bed as a child. There were a number of dreams in which he was urinating in inappropriate places, and one in which he was incontinent.

11. He is concerned about maintaining order in his class. In the dreams, his pupils repeatedly showed him disrespect and hostility, and behaved in a disorderly manner.

12. He likes teaching young adolescents. There were a large number of children of this age in his dreams. He said he finds them exuberant and charming.

13. He is not preoccupied with clothes. There were only an average number of references to clothing in his dreams. He said he is not at all clothes conscious and dresses very casually.

14. He likes working around the house and fixing and repairing things. There were many dreams in which he was doing this.

15. It bothers him to live in an untidy house or one that is in a state of disrepair. There were many dreams in which these concerns were expressed. He said it would bother him considerably to live in an untidy house.

16. He is not particularly close to his mother. His mother rarely entered his dreams.

17. He feels threatened by adult males. The dreamer was frequently the victim of attack by adult males.

18. He does not think of himself as being a strong, effective male. The dreamer is often unable to deal with situations effectively. He acknowledged that he has been concerned about his adequacy as a male many times.

19. He is not afraid of failing. There were few dreams in which he failed.

20. He does not feel completely mature. This prediction was made because he associates with many adolescents in his dreams. It might be objected that the reason he dreams of adolescents is that he associates with them all day in the classroom, and that it has nothing to do with his maturity or immaturity. To this objection we would reply that he very likely chose to teach this age group because he identifies himself with them. Tony admitted that he has never felt completely grown up.

21. He likes males better than females. In his dreams, he

had more friendliness with males than with females, which is contrary to the norms for male dreamers.

22. He does not feel that he can compete successfully with other males for attention and acceptance by women. He had dreams of being rejected by women who favored other men.

23. He prefers to be with young people more than with adults. Again the reason for making this prediction was the presence of a large number of minors in his dreams. He replied, "Without doubt, I prefer to be with young people rather than adults."

24. He is afraid of losing control of himself. He had dreams in which he gave in to his impulses. He said, "Yes, there have been many times when I was afraid of losing control of myself."

25. He has sometimes wanted to be a female. He had dreams of being a woman.

> I saw myself in the mirror. I was A.W. (a girl's name). I said, "Oh, I forgot I was a girl. But I don't have a hole down there." The friend I was with seemed surprised. I took down my underwear and showed him my penis, which was slightly bent and limp.

26. He was molested sexually as a young child. He had a dream in which he was seduced in a basement. In this dream, he saw himself as a child. In another dream, he was in the power of a huge giant who was going to eat him.

27. He is concerned about his sexual potency and virility as a male. There were dreams in which he was sexually inadequate.

28. He is not exclusively homosexual or heterosexual. In his dreams, he sometimes had sexual relations with males, and sometimes with females. In an account he wrote for us of his sexual experiences, he mentioned both males and females. His first sexual contact was with a boy when Tony was 16 years old. His first heterosexual experience was while he was in the service. Following this, there were some casual affairs with girls, and a four-year love affair with an adolescent boy. He has seduced other boys, and once was interrogated by the police for discussing masturbation with a 12-year-old boy. At the present time (1970) he is seriously involved with a young woman, and thinks his homosexual impulses are waning.

29. His preference is homosexuality. He had more homosexual than heterosexual dreams.

30. He prefers sexual relations with minors to those with adults. There were more dreams in which he was having sexual relations with adolescents than with adults.

31. He prefers boys to girls as sexual partners. There

were more dreams of sexual relations with boys than with girls. He admitted that he was attracted to adolescent boys. "There is something more desperate and exciting about sex with a boy."

32. He feels threatened by having sexual relations with adult females. There were dreams in which this feeling was expressed.

Six of the predictions we made were not confirmed by the answers Tony gave to our questions. We were particularly surprised by his categorical denial of a wish to wear women's clothes and an urge to exhibit himself sexually before his class, because he did both of these things in his dreams.

In summary, then, 32 of the 38 inferences (80 percent) we made about Tony's behavior and feelings were confirmed. If we were to characterize Tony's personality from his dreams, we would have to conclude that he is still an adolescent in many respects. His attraction to adolescent boys is motivated by his narcissistic desire to retain or regain his youth. As he grows older, it becomes more difficult for him to maintain this fiction. His house (body) is showing signs of age. We might say that Tony suffers from a Dorian Grey complex, after the story by Oscar Wilde (himself a lover of boys) of a man who wished to remain forever young and beautiful.

A twenty-year-old male sent us fifty dreams to be analyzed. In this case, we wanted to see how many correct predictions we could make from the quantitative results of the analysis alone, without using any qualitative judgments or symbolic interpretations. We compared the frequencies with which various elements appeared in his dreams with the frequencies obtained from the analysis of a large number of male dreams. The following predictions were confirmed by the dreamer.

1. He is more interested in indoor activities than outdoor activities. There were many more dreams in which the dreamer was indoors than outdoors. The typical young male dreams more of being in outdoor settings. The dreamer said he was almost entirely interested in indoor activities.

2. He spends more time indoors than outdoors. The basis for this prediction is the same as the foregoing one.

3. He is not interested in sports. There were few references to sports or sports equipment in his dreams.

4. He does not like to do manual work. Tools and manual activities were rarely mentioned in his dreams.

5. He is not interested in nature. Nature did not appear very often in his dreams.

6. He is not interested in doing household chores. There were few references to household articles.

7. He feels more secure when he is in the house than he does when he is on the street. There were many house settings and few street settings.

8. He feels fairly close to his family. Many members of his family came into his dreams.

9. He does not have many close friends. Few friends were mentioned in his dreams. He said he had only three close friends.

10. He has fairly strong aggressive impulses but they are restrained. There were many aggressive interactions in his dreams.

11. He does not get into many fights. Same reason as above.

12. He feels that he is more apt to be the victim of attack by others than to be the attacker. In his aggressive dreams he was more often the victim than the attacker.

13. He is afraid of being attacked. Same reason as above.

14. He feels males are more hostile than females are. He has more aggressions with males than with females in his dreams.

15. He feels that people are not usually friendly and helpful. There was more aggression than friendliness in his dreams.

16. He is preoccupied with sex in waking life but he has actually not had many sex experiences and is sexually frustrated. He had many sex dreams. He says he has never had any sexual experiences, and that he feels sexually frustrated.

17. He is concerned about money. There were many references to money in his dreams.

18. He is not interested in clothes. There were few mentions of clothes in his dreams. He says, "There is hardly any interest at all."

Among the four predictions that were not confirmed by the dreamer, one, in particular, surprised us. We thought the dreamer would be preoccupied with guns and other weapons in waking life because there were so many references to them in his dreams. His response was that he hated guns. This strong feeling suggests that it might be a reaction formation, and that he is afraid of his admittedly strong aggressive impulses.

Overall, then, the dreams portray the dreamer as feeling most secure and comfortable when he is with his family at home. He does not like manual or athletic activities, nor does he enjoy nature. He is not very sociable outside the family group. He is afraid of people and he is also afraid of sex. He has strong aggressive and sexual drives but they are either suppressed in waking life or find substitute outlets.

Another twenty-year-old who sent copies of his dreams was also tied to his family, but unlike the previous dreamer he was bitter and resentful toward them. The only person he felt close to was his six-year-old niece, who lived in the same house. He even dreamed of having sex with her, which is an indication of immaturity. There was a lot of regression in his dreams. He dreamed of his old home, of old friends he no longer saw, and former activities he had given up. This return to the "good old days" when life was a lot better is also a mark of immaturity. He is afraid to leave the security of his family although he resents them, and so he tries to escape into the past in his dreams.

He is sexually frustrated although preoccupied by sex, so he dreams a great deal about sex, which he has with both males and females. This dreamer, like so many other young people, is caught in the dependence-independence conflict. His dreams exhibit this quite distinctly, and it is confirmed by his behavior and feelings in waking life.

The next individual whose dreams we analyzed was a middle-aged businessman. From his dreams it was inferred that he was married, had two daughters in college, no sons, and that he himself was an only child—all of which was true. His chief hobby is stamp-collecting, of which he often dreamed. We could not determine what his business was because he never dreamed about his work. We inferred from his dreams that he had no close friends, because he never dreamed about any. This was true. Because of the large number of strangers in his dreams we thought he might feel alienated from people and from himself, but he said this was not the case. In view of other information obtained from his dreams and from him, we wonder whether alienation was not more of a problem than he realized.

His preoccupation with clothes, household furnishings, household chores like cooking and cleaning, and with children, suggested he had a feminine orientation. A low occurrence of tools and manual activities in his dreams supported this suggestion, which was later confirmed by the dreamer.

The feminine orientation was evidenced by his dreaming of wearing women's clothes. He was actually a transvestite in waking life. A number of predictions related to his feminine orientation and transvestism were made.

1. He has wanted to be a female. He wrote, "Yes, rather desperately so in my younger years, and the twinges still rack me once in a while."
2. He thinks of himself as being part male and part female. Here is one of his dreams.

I am at an exhibit on mankind. Focal point is a tall male mannikin dressed in mod clothes. The model is an exact copy of myself. Growing out of one part of the dummy is another head, closely resembling me also. But it is decidedly a feminine head.

In answering the questions we asked him, he would sometimes say, "C. [his feminine name] would answer it one way and I would answer it in another." He said he feels like "a male on the exterior and female inside."
3. He has wished he could give birth to a baby. Here is such a dream.

I enter a bar with a baby and I put her in a high chair. I have a feeling she is my daughter and I her mother.

He wrote to us, "Yes, I would like to have a baby if by some twist of magic I could find myself dressing, living, and being known as a woman."
4. He has considered having himself changed into a woman. He said he may have thought of this occasionally.
5. He dresses as a woman only in private. He states he has worn women's clothes in public several times but he now restricts cross-dressing to the privacy of his own home and only in the presence of his wife. She is, in fact, very cooperative and knew about his transvestism before their marriage. She does his hair for him and teaches him how to act more womanly. Apparently, they have a very congenial relationship.
6. He would be embarrassed to be seen dressed as a woman outside of his own home. There were a number of dreams of this type. This is one of them.

I am on a train. I look down and see I have on women's high heeled shoes. I am shocked at this and I am afraid some passengers might notice.

He said he would not be embarrassed. On the other hand, he never shows himself in public dressed as a woman, and he keeps it a secret from his daughters, his business associates, and his neighbors. They rarely have company and they have no close friends, so there is little chance of him being observed as a woman. One time a neighbor woman came in while he was wearing women's slacks and giving his wife a permanent, and he did not feel embarrassed.

7. He has had sexual relations with males, which is true.

8. He prefers masculine men like soldiers and sailors for sex, and he also prefers boys. Here are two dreams on which this inference was based.

> I am driving down a street. Ahead of me are some soldiers marching and I put on the brakes but I slip toward them and actually bump slightly several men in the back rank. They don't seem to mind.

> I am riding on a bus. Some young boys enter. One is sitting behind me and I feel a stick poke under the rear and I jump with a slight protest. Then a young boy carrying a new bullwhip sits down alongside me. He turns to me and I note his shirt is open and I poke him away and off the seat with a small stick which I push against his chest.

He acknowledged that he does prefer masculine men, but he says he is not attracted sexually to boys.

9. He has paid and been paid to have sexual relations with males. Our prediction was derived from this type of dream.

> I am attempting to buy a painting from a soldier. An officer shouts that he will shoot any soldier giving money to anyone. I decide to leave but first I give my calling card to the soldier and promise to pay him later.

This has never happened, so he said, but he admitted he might be willing to do so under the proper circumstances.

10. He has been approached sexually by males and sometimes he has said yes, and sometimes no. Here is one such dream.

> I am walking down a street with a man. He puts his hand on my fly. I protest, telling him that they arrest you for that in this city.

He has been approached but he has always said no. (And yet he confessed that he has performed homosexual acts.)

This case is instructive because it shows that a secret—or a set of related secrets—which he has guarded from everyone except his wife and a few transvestite acquaintances are fully expressed in his dreams. Despite the fact that he acts out some of these secrets in waking life, nevertheless he continues to dream about them. His dreams are his life, and his life are his dreams, except for one important difference. The facade that he presents to the public—what Jung called the *persona*—does not get into his dreams. It is only the very private sector of his life that does that. Nor is this secret life unconscious. It is fully conscious or very near to consciousness. He knows what he is and what he wants, and it did not take an analysis of his dreams to tell him. He regards himself as being fairly well adjusted. He says he enjoys his work, his family, and his hobbies. And yet, the interior woman feeling is always gnawing at him.

Karl, an engineer in his early thirties, began keeping a record of his dreams in January, 1968 and has been providing us with copies of them ever since that date. He is a prolific recaller of dreams and over the three-year period has recorded over a thousand dreams. From the mass of information we have secured from the analysis of his dreams, we have selected four recurrent themes to discuss because they illustrate what appears to be a lack of continuity between dreams and waking life. As we shall see, the lack of continuity is more apparent than real. The four topics are sex, violent aggression, athletics, and dreams of his boyhood home.

Karl has many passionate sex dreams which are usually described in vivid and uninhibited detail although, surprisingly, none of them results in a nocturnal emission. Here are a few examples.

M. gets up on a table. I kiss and fondle her. Now I am caressing her vulva with my tongue and lips. I move into a regular pattern; she attains orgasm. It's wild. We then have intercourse.

S. and I are now violently loving each other, copulating with enthusiasm. Her vaginal grip and muscle control are terrific. She is really reaching ecstacy. I am also. Intercourse ends majestically.

Over a three-year period he has had sexual relations in his dreams with 38 different women, many of them repeatedly, and with two males. Most of his sexual partners are women he knows and to whom he has been attracted in waking life.

Karl was married when he was in his early twenties. At the time of his marriage he was a virgin. When we asked him why he had never had premarital sex, he replied, "I remained a virgin before marriage because, at the time, I felt premarital intercourse was categorically an immoral and unintelligent thing to engage in."

From the beginning of his marriage, his wife did not satisfy him sexually and soon became a source of considerable sexual frustration. She did not like any foreplay activites, refused to kiss sensually or to have her breasts stimulated, and would not permit, except under provocation, any deviation from the conventional sexual position. Karl says of her rather bitterly, "Not once in our marriage has she warmly initiated intercourse. She has never come over and touched me anywhere, put her arm around me, or done anything by touch to show desire for me." As a consequence of her coldness, so he says, Karl is often impotent when they have intercourse.

Yet, in spite of this unhappy state of affairs, Karl did not have extramarital intercourse until he separated from his wife after twelve years of marriage (they were later divorced), and then he had only one sexual encounter with a woman. Moreover, for several years prior to their separation, his wife urged him to have affairs with women because, as she said, she was not satisfying him sexually. It is also interesting that she urged him to have a vasectomy which he did.

Given these deplorable circumstances, it is not surprising that Karl is preoccupied with sex both in his waking life and in his dreams. His one outlet is masturbation, which he indulges in once or twice a day. (For a married man of Karl's age, the frequency of masturbation is about once a month, according to the Kinsey studies.) This is accompanied by vivid sexual fantasies. He has never engaged in a homosexual act.

Karl's masturbation fantasies are an exact counterpart of his nocturnal dreams. In that sense, there is continuity between dreams and waking life.

It is an interesting psychological question why a man who has ample opportunity for sexual experiences, who is physically healthy and extremely well-built, and who has his wife's encouragement to obtain pleasure from other women should prefer masturbation to sexual intercourse. His dreams and information obtained from him help to provide an answer to this question.

Karl is very conscious of his body, and through regular

exercise, weight-lifting and jogging, and proper nutrition he has become a giant of a man. He is six feet, two inches tall and weighs 240 pounds. He recognizes that this emphasis on body-building and physical fitness is a compensation for feelings of physical inferiority, from which he suffered intensely as a boy. His overdeveloped body also helped to compensate for an undersized penis.

Despite his present splendid physique he still feels inferior when he compares himself to other men. He subscribes to two weight-lifting magazines and enjoys looking at the pictures of lifters performing. "I am conscious of my own body, especially proportions and symmetry. I admire a strong, lean male physique and I am occupied with methods of developing one." His present body is massive rather than lean. His dreams also contain a number of references to physical disability, heart attacks, and death.

We suspect that Karl feels sex with women might weaken his virility and would be debilitating and injurious to his health. Loss of semen is often equated with loss of strength (the Samson complex?). Also, men of this type are often unconsciously afraid that sex with women may result in castration. It is significant perhaps that none of Karl's sex dreams results in nocturnal emission, and many of them are interrupted prior to climax. Others are unsatisfactory. Masturbation, on the other hand, always leads to orgasm.

A person with a lot of body narcissism (love of one's body) is often unwilling to share his body with another person. His preference is for masturbation.

It is significant, in this connection, that Karl's physical activities are solitary ones, such as weight-lifting and jogging, and not group or contact sports. His sexual activities are also primarily solitary. Building a strong outstanding erect body by exercise is not unlike bringing the penis to erection by manipulation.

Karl's ambivalence toward his body is indicated by dreaming about leaving his body, as in this example.

With each succeeding dream I come closer to leaving the body as in astral projection. Each dream seems to be an awakening deeper and deeper into projection. My struggles to free myself from the body each time are terrific.

One might wonder why a person who has devoted so much time to developing his body should want to leave it.

Karl has many violent and sadistic dreams of the following sort.

> J. W. makes a discourteous remark. We end up in a fight and I shred him, really reduce him to ruins, knocked several teeth out, his face is bleeding.

> A woman is a prisoner and has shackles on her wrist. She is required to do a lot of hard work and is chained to a chair when she is not working. She is hungry, thirsty, tormented, about to go insane. Occasionally she is tortured by those holding her prisoner.

> I'm in a strange city in bright daylight. My dad is across the street. I shoot him with a high-caliber rifle. I think he is dead. He gets up again. I shoot him again. This time he is dead.

Yet, in waking life he is not of a violent nature, never gets in fights, and regards himself as being a friendly, warmhearted, peaceful person.

Actually, he is not all that friendly. Over and over again, in answering questions we asked him, he expressed hatred for his father and resentment toward his mother and wife. He quit football in his freshman year at the university partially to get even with his father who derived considerable pleasure from his son's exploits on the gridiron. Karl wrote to us of this episode: "The sorry bastard was all set to soak up the old glory at my expense. No sooner was he all situated [his father had become active in the quarterback club and had been elected president of the alumni association] than I slipped out of the situation that May. It really left him high and dry, really frosted his ass. It was great, a real pleasure."

Karl repeatedly dreamed of playing football. He was an outstanding player in high school and won a football scholarship from a major university. He quit playing after the first season. Since then he says he has taken no interest in the game and never watches it. Why, then, should he dream about it so often?

Is it to make restitution to his father? There is no evidence in his dreams or waking life to support a positive answer to this question. He still resents his father as much as he ever did.

Does it represent a return to happier times when he enjoyed having aggressive, physical contact with other males? There is much to suggest that he did enjoy this aspect of the game. He wrote to us as follows: "I was an offensive end as a freshman and was never the least hesitant to clobber people. One block I threw from scrimmage knocked a defensive tackle unconscious. I prefer head-on collisions in high traffic areas where I can corner or channel a runner and get a solid shot." Football seems to have provided one outlet for his violent aggression.

Physical contact with males may also have had an erotic element associated with it. Karl does associate aggression with sex, and he has had homosexual dreams such as the following one:

(He is looking at a picture catalogue which is like a pornographic sex manual. He turns the pages.)
I find a full-page photo of a male figure with wings. The man is very well built. Then the page becomes life-size. As erotic feeling rises, the man comes to life. He is lying opposite me in a posture headed in the opposite direction. The man's penis now goes into full erection, and I commence orally stimulating it. The man's mouth has already closed over mine. Mutual oral masturbation proceeds to orgasm in both of us.

Reaction formations to aggression and homosexuality may have been partially responsible for Karl's abandoning football and other contact sports, and retreating into solitary activities like weight-lifting and masturbation.

Actually, Karl has never given up an interest in football. Somewhat reluctantly he admitted to us that in 1963 he made a serious effort to be taken on by a major football club but was not accepted. He says that even now (1970) he would work out with a professional team if given the opportunity. "Who knows, maybe I'm kidding myself about not liking football. Perhaps I do, and don't want to admit it. I don't really know, but there's some sort of hang-up rooted in it."

Karl's athletic dreams, 65 in all, were about equally divided between failure and success. When he failed, it was often an abysmal failure; when he succeeded, it was often a dazzling success. In these dreams, the wish to be an outstanding athlete was pitted against the fear of failure. His abandonment of all competitive sports in waking life suggests that the fear overrode the wish. And yet of all Karl's dreams, those in which he is engaging in competitive athletics contain the highest proportion of satisfying experiences. It seems that he gave up a rewarding activity to spite his father, or for other reasons.

The fourth recurrent topic in Karl's dreams is dreaming about being back in the family home where his mother now lives alone. She divorced Karl's father when Karl was 13. Karl continued to live with his mother and two brothers until he graduated from high school and entered the university. Since his marriage he visits his mother infrequently, no more than once or twice a year, and then only out of a sense of duty. He says that his childhood years were unhappy, and he cannot understand why he should dream so frequently of his old home where he had so many unpleasant experiences. He thinks the earlier days may have been happier ones than the present because there was "some hope" then, which there is not now. If this were correct then the regression in his dreams would be motivated by a desire to retreat from a more undesirable present to a less undesirable past.

When we examined the 99 dreams in which Karl dreamed of being back at his boyhood home, we found that only eight of them contained any pleasurable features. Most of the dreams were filled with irritation, anger, aggression, fear, frustration, depression, sadness, and anxiety. For instance, he dreamed a man was entering the house intending to kill him. In another dream, he was making the house more secure by installing new locks. In these boyhood home dreams, resentment and hostility toward his wife and mother predominated over anger toward his father and brothers by a margin of four to one. In one dream, his mother dies and he feels relief. In another dream, his father dies of a heart attack following which the dreamer has a heart attack. When he dreams he is married to his mother, he feels depressed and bitter. He hates his mother in a dream because she intrudes while he and his wife are having sexual relations. In another dream, his wife intrudes when Karl is having sex with a woman friend.

In many of these old home dreams, there is something wrong with the house or it is in danger of being destroyed. Karl sets fire to the house in one dream. There are also dreams in which the dreamer is working around the house or yard. In several dreams, he is mowing the lawn. Karl thinks these dreams of mowing the grass represent "getting things over with" so he could do something he enjoyed. He also mentioned that his father demanded that he do things well, like cutting the grass. Actually, another dream revealed to us the meaning of mowing the grass. In this dream, some person

suggests to Karl that he can use hypnosis to supplant masturbation with trimming the grass. The dreamer agrees to try it.
"After trimming a while I find, under hypnosis, that I'm near-
ing orgasm."

Certainly there is very little ambivalence in these "old
home" dreams. The dreamer has few positive, happy feelings
associated with his boyhood home, yet he continues to dream
about it more frequently than any other setting. One cannot
take too seriously his explanation that there was still hope
when he lived there. His dreams reflect much more hopeless-
ness than hope.

What seems to be evident is that Karl is still burdened by
the memories of a painful boyhood, and these memories
exercise an oppressive influence on his present life. Even
though he stays away from his old home in waking life, he is
often unhappily there in his dreams. For Karl, there is no
escape, not even in his dreams, from a painful past.

In one of the dream series we analyzed, there was a very
low incidence of sex dreams. This surprised us because the
dreamer is a vigorous, attractive young man in his early
twenties. Since he had only recently been married, the low
incidence of sex dreams might be attributed to adequate
sexual satisfaction in waking life. In reality, he has intercourse with his wife only about once a week. He has no other
sexual outlets except with her. This frequency is far below
the average number of outlets established by the Kinsey
studies of human sexuality. In other words, the low incidence
of sex dreams reflected the waking reality.

The dreamer acknowledged that he was "not all that
interested in sex." He felt that his sexual energy was expend-
ed in strenuous physical activities, especially surfing, whose
erotic symbolism he recognized. About it he wrote, "The
trick of surfing is to insert the phallic surfboard into the
hollow vagina-shaped portion of an ocean wave which is
known as the *tube*."

This same dreamer had a large number of references to
food and eating in his dreams. In his daytime diary, which
paralleled his dream diary, he usually detailed what he had
eaten during the day. He is also somewhat of a food faddist.

The evidence presented in this chapter substantiates the
continuity hypothesis. There is considerable congruence between what a person dreams about at night and what he does
or thinks about when he is awake. The distinction between
doing and thinking (or fantasying) enables us to reconcile

the continuity hypothesis with the popular idea that dreams compensate for desires which remain unfulfilled in waking life. We have observed that a person who has many sex dreams may have few sexual outlets, aside from masturbation, in waking life. (But it is also true that a person may have many sexual experiences in reality and also have many sex dreams.) In this sense, dreams do compensate for something a person lacks in everyday life. He does not, however, lack sexual thoughts and fantasies, of which he has an abundance. These fantasies may accompany rather frequent masturbation.

An inverse relationship between dreams and actual deeds, and a positive relationship between dreams and imagined deeds seems to apply primarily to sex and aggression, and then only for some individuals. For other individuals there is a positive relationship between dream deeds and actual deeds in the realm of sex and aggression. In virtually all other aspects of life that we have examined, there is a close correspondence between dreams and actual behavior.

Occasionally, our predictions from dreams of what a person either does or thinks were not confirmed because the person was unaware of his own behavior. In one instance, we predicted that a man who dreamed more often of being the aggressor than the victim was more likely to take the initiative in being aggressive in waking life. He said this was not true. Later, he wrote to us and said he had been observing his reactions and discovered that he usually was the aggressor.

Sometimes our predictions failed because the person was reluctant to admit something. Karl who dreamed repeatedly about playing football said, at first, he had lost interest in the game but later confessed that he still wanted to play. Sometimes our predictions were not confirmed because of the way in which the question was worded. Few people, we discovered, are willing to admit to being unfriendly, undersexed, sadistic, or lacking in affection.

We have learned that, when the dreams clearly say one thing and the dreamer says something different, to trust the dreams and not the dreamer. In this connection, we had an amusing experience in predicting something from a single dream. A young married woman of our acquaintance who was pregnant told us a dream. The gist of the dream is as follows. She and her husband were skiing down a hill when they came to a road where a large woman, who was holding a child by the hand, was trying to get into a wagon. She asked the dreamer and her husband to help her, which they did reluctantly because it interrupted their skiing.

We asked the dreamer whether she had any younger brothers or sisters, because our inference was that the dream referred to a time when the dreamer was a child and her mother had been pregnant. Just as the dreamer's present sexual relations with her husband were interrupted by her pregnancy (which she acknowledged was the case), so we thought her pleasurable relationship with her mother had been interfered with by the mother's pregnancy, and the subsequent birth of a competing brother or sister. She said she had no younger sibling. A little later in our conversation we were discussing twins and whether there was any possibility she might give birth to twins. She said there might be because her mother had had twins. We asked whether they had been born after her and she said they had. When confronted with the obvious contradiction between her earlier statement and the present one, she said she had forgotten about the twins because they had died while they were quite young. Her dream did not forget.

Dreams do not lie.

Chapter 7

Symbolism in Dreams
and Waking Life

In a previous chapter we dealt with the question of symbols in dreams. In this chapter we will discuss the relation of symbolism in dreams to symbolism in everyday life. Our thesis, simply stated, is that even the most prosaic object or activity in waking life is symbolic to some degree, and that an analysis of the role an object or activity plays in dreams will shed light on its metaphorical significance in waking life. We believe there is a direct correlation between dream symbolism and waking symbolism. If symbolization is present in dreams, then it is also present in waking life. It is also our contention that there is much more symbolism in everyday life than we realize. The study of dreams helps us to recognize the pervasiveness of metaphorical symbols in our daily life.

For the most part, a person perceives objects in his dreams in the same way as he does in waking life. Windows are looked out of or into, beds are slept in, automobiles are driven, newspapers are read, canoes are paddled, doors are opened or closed, sidewalks are walked on, food is bought, cooked, served, and eaten, knives cut, guns shoot, rooms are entered, bridges are crossed, clothes are purchased and worn, airplanes fly, mountains are climbed, elevators ascend or descend, teeth are extracted, chairs are sat on, luggage is packed, lights are turned on and off, pictures are looked at, tires go flat, the sun shines, cigarettes are smoked, trees are climbed, and letters are mailed.

As a general rule, the objects that appear in dreams are the objects of waking life with which the dreamer is familiar, and the frequency with which they appear in dreams corresponds to the dreamer's familiarity with them. For persons living in urban communities in the United States, the ten most common objects are house, room, automobile, street, door, stairs, building, water, floor, and table in that order. For people living in a completely different environment, other objects would be found in their dreams but they would still be objects with which they were familiar in waking life. Australian aborigines, for instance, dream frequently of boats, rivers, fishing, spears, making camp, and yams, which are familiar objects and activities in their lives. The physical environment in dreams quite accurately reflects the physical environment in waking life.

In the chapter on dream symbolism we said that one criterion for recognizing a symbol in a dream was the appearance of an unusual object, or a peculiar type of activity. For example, a man dreamed that his wife was carrying a walking stick and flaunted it in an arrogant, domineering way. Although walking sticks exist, they are rarely used in the United States except by elderly or disabled people. The dreamer's wife never used one. His mother carried a cane, and this may have been the reason for its appearance in the dream. Moreover, she sometimes brandished her cane in an ostentatious and domineering manner at oncoming traffic when she started to cross the street. The dreamer attributed to his wife in the dream an object that his mother actually used. His wife flaunted it just as his mother had. The stick symbolized the dreamer's conception of his wife.

In another dream, the dreamer himself was swinging a cane and accosted a male friend in an offensive manner. In this dream, he was playing the role of the domineering male, which the cane accentuated. If we say that the walking stick or cane symbolizes masculinity, then we see in these two dreams a phallic, castrating female and a phallic, castrating male. In the first dream, the dreamer identified his wife with his mother, who in reality was a very dominant woman; in the second, the dreamer identified himself with his mother.

For every instance of an unusual object in dreams, there are a hundred instances of quite ordinary objects being used in quite ordinary ways. Consider the following pair of dreams. In one of them, the dreamer is given a big cigar by another man. In the other, he observes a man buying a large Western-style hat, and decides to buy one for himself. There is nothing unusual about cigars or hats, nor is it strange that the dreamer should be given a cigar or want a hat. We might leave it at that and say that cigars are cigars and hats are hats, whether in dreams or in waking life. Suppose, however, we assume that cigars and hats are phallic symbols. In that case, their acquisition in dreams represents a wish for more impressive genitals. If this is correct in dreams, then their acquisition in waking life represents the same wish. We would even extend our argument by saying that cigars and hats were invented in the first place out of a desire for phallic enhancement.

Parenthetically, it should be pointed out that cigars and hats have other symbolic meanings. A cigar is put in the mouth and sucked, just as the breast is put in the mouth and sucked. Tipping a hat to a woman could sometimes mean a sexual invitation. Since the hat protects the head, it could be interpreted as a shield against danger (castration?). We believe many of the common objects in our environment have multiple symbolic significance. That is, an object can symbolize several things at the same time.

Recall the dream of the faucet. We had no difficulty deciphering the faucet as a phallic symbol because when it was turned on by the female plumber, the young man was also "turned on." The faucet is a commonplace object which everyone uses a number of times each day. The dreamer probably used it before going to bed that night. There may even have been something wrong with it. It is not inconceivable that the resemblance between his penis and the faucet flashed through his mind, and later, while he was asleep and dreaming, his penis was transformed into a faucet.

Why do such things as faucets exist in the world? Obviously someone had to invent the faucet, since it is not a natural object like a tree or a lake. Why was it invented? The usual answer is that it was invented to serve the useful function of controlling the flow of water out of a pipe. The faucet dream suggests that there may be another answer in addition to the conventional one. The inventor of the faucet may have been motivated by a desire for a better penis, one that he could turn on and off at will. That his fantasy of a better organ proved to have useful consequences could have been the result and not the cause of his invention.

In our discussion of dreams containing references to prenatal life, we said they consisted of wishes to return to the pleasures and protection of fetal existence, and fears of being smothered or squashed in the womb. Out of these same wishes and fears man constructs better wombs in his waking life. Take, for example, the almost universal custom of living in an enclosure. A house is like a womb, but it is an improved womb. It is easy to leave and easy to enter, so that inside and outside dangers can be avoided. The dream of not being able to get back in the house, which is a fairly common one, is especially terrifying because the dreamer is exposed to danger. A house is roomy and can be shared with others. A house has eyes in the form of windows. Some houses have second and third stories and porches from which the world can be viewed from a safe vantage point.

The evolution of living enclosures from cave to castle reveals the improvement that has been made by man in his womblike residences. The stages of this evolution can still be seen in some Spanish villages, where some people still live in hillside caves. (Caves also occur in dreams.) Some of these caves have roofs over the entrances, which enlarges the living area. Walls are then built to make the first room. An opening is made for a door and windows are added. Eventually the cave is abandoned and the house is enlarged. Water, gas, and electricity are piped into the house, which makes it more self-contained, and furniture is introduced which makes it more comfortable. Even the evolution of furniture from rough, hard benches and beds to soft and enveloping chairs and beds shows the trend toward a more comfortable womblike existence. The house is connected to the outside world by telephone, radio, and television. Refrigerators and freezers make fewer trips outside necessary. Houses of the future will probably contain a garden under glass with controlled temperature so that the occupants can produce their own food.

Yet with all these improvements, people who remain indoors for very long complain of being "cooped up." They develop claustrophobia. This causes restiveness, quarreling, and much moving around, particularly in the United States where people change their residence almost as often as they change cars. The point is that they are never satisfied because a house is not a womb and never can be. It appears what people really want is a womblike atmosphere without the fears associated with the original womb. This they can never have. A common anxiety dream is one in which the dreamer's dwelling is broken into by robbers or killers. Another is of being chased by an enemy and not being able to get into one's house.

Even the parts of a house possess symbolic significance. Here is a dream involving a door. A young man dreamed of being in a house with a girl to whom he was attracted. She left the room and he followed her. She entered the bathroom and closed the door. He opened the door and at that moment had an orgasm. Recall in this connection the young man who dreamed of entering the port of a spaceship. The symbolism of the door in the following dream seems to be self-evident.

> I wanted to buy a watch but I didn't have enough money. After leaving by the rear door, I found a roll of bills in a dung heap and hid it for fear it would be taken from me.

The body imagery in the next dream also seems to be transparent.

> The front door was open. A stream of water from the garden hose came in through the open door, striking my bed. I was in my nightgown and knew I must go out and shut off the water. It didn't occur to me to shut the door. My bed was getting wetter and wetter.

Consider the window. During a ten-year period, a man recorded 43 dreams in which a window was mentioned. In 21 of these dreams the dreamer was looking through a window. In 10, another person was looking through a window. The dreamer looked out of and into windows equally often, but the other persons always looked in and never out of windows. Moreover, they were always looking in at the dreamer, and most of the time, they saw the dreamer engaged in some sexual activity.

The dreamer also used the window to spy upon other people, and in five of the dreams he was watching people have sexual relations. The window appears to be a voyeuristic symbol—"the eye of the house." It may even have been invented for this purpose as well as for light and ventilation. The first person who cut a hole in the side of his house may have wanted to look out and see what was going on. But a window that can be looked out of can also be looked into; hence the desire to watch is counteracted by the fear of being watched. That is one reason why there are window shades (eyelids?).

Dreams of attics, basements, closets, and bathrooms are often richly symbolic, and seem to be metaphorical in waking life as well. A man dreamed that the roof of a house had been damaged, and plans were being made to reroof it. He had this dream shortly before he was to undergo an operation on his brain.

Let us turn to another favorite dream object, the automobile. What symbolic significance has been attributed to the automobile in waking life? Status, power and speed, and sex are the principal features that are emphasized in advertising. (These features are not unrelated.) The car serves as a sex symbol in several ways. Any extension of the body that protrudes as the hood of a car does may be regarded as phallic enhancement. The car's power enhances the driver's potency. The driver manipulates the wheel and steers in and out of traffic and through narrow spaces and parks the car in a garage. The phallic qualities have not gone unnoticed by car manufacturers and advertisers. Different models bear the names of virile-sounding wild animals or potent weapons.

Less obvious, perhaps, is the womblike character of the automobile. It is an enclosed space that can be entered and left. The car is hermaphroditic (a phallic womb), as are most conveyances, from the airplane to the submarine. The automobile obliterates the differentiation into male and female that resulted, according to legend, from a splitting of an originally hermaphroditic being. It also reunited mother and child. It overcomes the father by the driver becoming a more masculinized person. Anything that serves to satisfy these three basic desires—for the merging of male and female, for reunion with the mother, and for overcoming father—is certainly a potent symbol, awake or asleep.

Symbols satisfy but they may also terrify. The automobile is a dangerous machine, to which mounting traffic accidents and fatalities testify. One runs grave risks in acting out fantasies of bisexuality, incest, and parricide. Wish and fear are opposite sides of the same coin.

In order to demonstrate the symbolic significance of automobiles in dreams, we examined 77 automobile dreams that a man recorded over a ten-year period. He had 652 dreams during this time, so an automobile occurred in about every twelfth dream.

Themes of destruction and obstruction predominated. In 25 dreams, there was a threatened accident or an actual accident. Cars skidded, ran off the road, plunged over cliffs, overturned, caught fire, collided, and struck objects or pedestrians. In ten of the 25 dreams, the accident or near-accident was the fault of the driver, in ten it was due to an external condition, and in the other five it resulted from a mechanical defect.

In 21 dreams, an automobile was unable to proceed or to reach its destination. It was stopped by a traffic light, halted by the police, had a flat tire, lost a wheel, ran out of gas, lacked power, or encountered an obstacle. In nine of these obstruction dreams, the cause was a defect in the car, in ten the obstacle was an external one, and in two the driver was at fault.

From one point of view, these automobile dreams reflect the actual circumstances of waking life. Cars *do* run out of gas, skid, have flat tires, run off the road, encounter obstacles, collide, and get stopped by the police. One can take the usual point of view, that experiences of the day provide material for dreams of the night. Or one can invert this viewpoint and state that dreams of the night reveal meaning of events of the day. If a married man dreams he is driving with a woman other than his wife, and the car skids off the road and narrowly avoids plunging over a cliff (an actual dream), there would be no serious objection to interpreting this as a guilt dream. The man is punishing himself for being unfaithful to his wife.

Guilt may also be a contributing cause of accidents in waking life. If a man dreams that his car is endangered by a large truck, this may represent the dreamer's fear of his father's vengeance. If this explanation is correct for dreams, should it not also be correct for one's apprehension of large trucks in everyday life? If a tire becomes flat, a battery goes dead, or the engine stalls, may this not symbolize a person's feelings of impotence whether it appears in a dream or in waking life? May not a policeman, a traffic light, a curb, or a roadblock represent restrictive authority? If a car is a sex symbol, as everyone seems to agree, does it stretch belief too far to conjecture that an engine on fire symbolizes the flames of passion? It may be objected that engines do catch on fire for "natural" reasons, which have nothing to do with the sexual thoughts of the dreamer. We would not be willing to concede that point until it was established that the driver did not unconsciously contribute to the fire by the manner in which he operated or maintained the car. Upon analysis, "accidents" frequently turn out to have been unconsciously planned by the victim.

Even in the case of authentic accidents, the driver often feels guilty, although he may be blameless. Unconsciously, he feels he is being punished for something even though he cannot identify what it is.

In 12 of the 77 automobile dreams, a sexual activity took place in a car. The car is not an unusual place for sex to occur in waking life. It might be regarded as a convenient place for sexual relations, instead of inferring from these 12 dreams that the car is a sex symbol. It could be pointed out that sexual relations take place even more commonly in bed. Does that make the bed a sex symbol? We think so. "Going to bed with someone" or "sleeping together" are euphemisms for having sexual intercourse. The bed may even have been invented partially to facilitate erotic activities.

If the car is a sex symbol, it would tend to facilitate the expression of the sex drive, and even act as a stimulant to whet the sex impulse. Advertisers have exploited this message *ad nauseam.*

Speaking of advertising, it is commonly believed that advertisements plant ideas in the public mind. The car would not be a sex symbol unless advertising had made it so. We do not believe this. Advertising utilizes ideas and feelings that already exist; it does not ordinarily create new ones. Advertisements have just become less reticent in recent years about exploiting the vast appeal of sex.

Finally, there were 19 dreams in which the automobile played a neutral or miscellaneous role. The neutral dreams were those in which the car was either a passive part of the scenery or it was being used simply for transportation. In several dreams, the car was associated with pleasant activities. Pleasantries were exchanged between people in different cars, the dreamer was going to an amusement park with a friend, and the dreamer was in a car listening to music which moved him deeply. Some of the other dreams in the miscellaneous category contained the following events: while driving home the dreamer remembered he had left his hat at a friend's house, an automobile contained a corpse, and the dreamer was throwing coins from a car.

This type of analysis shows that the automobile may appear in dreams in numerous ways. This fact precludes assigning any fixed and universal symbolism, such as car=penis. In over half the dreams, the car is either a threat to the dreamer or it is frustrating him. It appears that man, having invented the car to satisfy basic wishes, discovers that the result of his invention is an increase in anxiety and frustration. One is reminded of the Hindu legend of the Juggernaut. Krishna (a father figure?) was drawn on a chariot under the wheels of which his fanatical followers (sons?) threw themselves and were crushed to death.

One lesson to be learned from the principal roles that the automobile plays in dreams is that man's attempt to enhance his power and potency by the invention of machines calls forth a counteraction of guilt and neurotic anxiety: guilt for having tried to surpass father and neurotic anxiety because the automobile arouses erotic and possibly incestuous impulses. The driver can lose control of a car, which happens in dreams and in waking life. The car is not dependable. It can and does break down and loses its power. The urge to buy new models may be largely motivated by a desire to replace an aging sex symbol with a fresh, vigorous one.

Let us consider another object, the bridge, which is the setting for a number of dreams. The bridge is a structure that connects two regions which are separated by water or some other impediment. The bridge as a symbol has attracted many writers. It has also figured in myths, legends, and initiation rites. One of the earliest games that children play is "London Bridge is Falling Down." The head of the Roman Catholic church is called pontiff (bridge-maker) because he builds bridges between heaven and earth.

What do bridges represent in dreams? We examined a number of dreams in which a bridge appeared and found a variety of conceptions represented. There is a bridge that falls just after the dreamer has crossed it. This suggests that there is no turning back for the dreamer. To emphasize her feeling of being cut off from the past, the road she has been traveling on after crossing the bridge collapses behind her.

More often, it is not the bridge that falls but someone or something falls from the bridge. In one dream, it was a train, and in several dreams, the dreamer fell from the bridge.

Bridges are also hazardous in waking life. They sometimes do fall down, and they are fallen from usually in a car. Bridges have a fatal attraction for people contemplating suicide. The Golden Gate Bridge in San Francisco is the scene of one suicide a month.

The bridge as a symbol of transition is suggested in several dreams. A young woman was refused passage across a bridge because she did not have a passport. The passport may be a symbol of maturity. A young man started across a bridge when it began to hail, so he ran back and took refuge in a shed. He, too, was not old enough to make the transition to maturity.

Freudians see the bridge as a symbol of sexual intercourse. One of our bridge dreams appears to carry a sexual connotation. The dreamer and another young man were out walking when they saw a large snake crawling in a crevice in a cliff. They returned to their car and the dreamer got a gun and filled his pocket with bullets. On the way back to where the snake was seen, they went through a covered bridge.

> I began to fondle the rifle and the bullets in my pocket. I loaded the rifle and started to laugh. We got back to the cliff and I saw the snake again. I fired the rifle and it did not go off, but the snake suddenly seemed to split in two.

There may also be sexual symbolism in two dreams in which young women fell into the water from a bridge. In both cases, they were with boyfriends. In one of the dreams, the bridge opened and they fell into the water. In the other dream, the dreamer and her boyfriend were on their honeymoon. They were driving fast, much to the dreamer's dismay, and crashed through a siderail of a bridge into deep water.

In legend and fairy tale, notably *Three Billy Goats Gruff*, what lies under a bridge is often treacherous and foul. This conception is also represented in dreams. A female dreamer was pushed from a bridge into a dark, muddy room underneath the bridge where she was held captive by black men.

We see in these bridge dreams a variety of conceptions which have their counterparts in waking life. The bridge as an embodiment of a desire to unite two separated bodies or to make a transition to maturity is counteracted by a fear of achieving such a union or of growing up.

The dream as *experienced* by the dreamer is a succession of images, and the dream as *reported* by the dreamer is a succession of words. In waking life, language is also the chief medium for describing one's thoughts, feelings, and fantasies. Words are not only denotative symbols, they are also metaphorical. In order to discover the metaphorical significance of a word it is usually necessary to study its history or etymology. If there is a close correlation between symbolism in dreams and symbolism in waking life, then the metaphorical

meaning of a dream image should be the same as the metaphorical meaning of the word used to describe that image.

In our analysis of the dream symbolism of windows, we
concluded that the window was the "eye of the house." We
did not know at the time that the last two letters of window
is derived from an old Norse word which means eye.

A college girl dreamed she went with her boyfriend to a
dance. He brought her a carnation. They entered the ballroom in high spirits, attracting everyone's attention. To her
chagrin the dreamer saw bloodstains on her white evening
gown, and found that blood dripped from the carnation. The
flower was bleeding! They left the ballroom in great embarrassment.

The etymology of the word *carnation* suggests that this
dream refers either to menstruation or to defloration. Carnation is derived from the Latin *carnis,* meaning flesh. Other
words from the same root are *carnal* and *incarnation.* The
flesh was bleeding and staining her purity and virginity, as
represented by the white dress. The reader may be interested
in looking up the etymology of another flower name, the
orchid, a flower which is given by a man to a woman as a
token of affection.

Slang is especially rich in metaphor, and many slang expressions are related to dream symbols. Recall the faucet
dream. A synonym for faucet is *cock,* and cock is a favorite
slang word for penis. The lady plumber turned on the dreamer's cock and semen flowed. The different ways in which the
word cock is used in polite speech also points to its phallic
significance. It refers to

> a male chicken or bird
> a weathervane in the shape of a rooster
> leader, chief, or head person
> hammer of a firearm
> a jaunty, erect position, as the cock of a hat
> raise stiffly, as a dog cocks its ears

We did the following study of the relation of slang to
dream symbols. We went through a dictionary of slang and
noted every expression for the male and female genitals.
There were 200 such terms for the male, and 330 for the
female. These expressions were classified under a number of
headings. A long list of dream symbols for the sex organs
were obtained from standard psychoanalytic writings, and

they were classified in the same way as the slang words were.

The largest class of slang words and dream symbols consisted of resemblances in shape between the metaphor and its referent. Examples of slang for the penis are stick, club, key, rod, pole, pencil, and poker. All of these expressions have their counterparts in dreams. (Etymologically, pencil is supposed to have been derived from the Latin word for "little penis.") The same is true of slang terms for the vagina such as ring, bag, box and pot. Phallic words and dream images have the qualities of length and hardness, whereas the female metaphors stress the container-like character of the vagina. That we associate two things in our mind by virtue of some resemblance is a principle of mental functioning that was known to Aristotle.

Implements and machinery constitute a large class of phallic slang and dream symbols, but a small one of metaphors for the vagina. *Tool* has been a favorite expression for the male member since the middle of the sixteenth century, and was even standard English until the eighteenth century. Shakespeare used the word in a sexual sense in *Henry VIII*. "Have we some strange Indian with the great tool come to court, the women so besiege us? Bless me, what a fry of fornication is at the door!" ("Fry of fornication" is an amusing play on words. *Fry* refers to recently hatched fish, and is derived from an old French word meaning "to spawn.")

Tools in dream symbolism are not difficult to find. Here is an example from a dream reported by an older woman. In her dream, she was entertaining a group of women in her apartment when the plumbing became stopped up. One of the women happened to have a plumber's snake in her purse!

It looked like a long, ten foot stiff chain encased in canvas. She got down on her knees and inserted the tool into a wall plug. She twisted and twisted it until most of the length was in the opening. I was enthralled and got down on the floor beside her and pulled it out. I told my aunt that is what I wanted for Christmas.

Among slang words for the penis there is only one that refers to a building or enclosure (skyscraper), but there are 28 such references for the female genitals. The same difference prevails in dreams. Enclosures, buildings, and especially houses have always been considered to have feminine connotations.

Twenty slang words for the penis have aggressive overtones, for instance, club, gun, and spear. Half as many words for the vagina are aggressive in character, for instance, bite, trap and catcher. It will be noted that the quality of shape differentiates within this category of aggressive words. It is improbable that the word *trap* would ever be used to denote the penis or that *gun* would ever be considered appropriate for the vagina.

Notice also the difference in the aggressive character of a trap and a gun. A trap catches and holds something, as a man is said to be trapped into marriage by a woman ("the tender trap"). A trap also has teeth and bites its victim. One of the oldest conceptions of the vagina is that it had teeth (*vagina dentata*) which clamped down on the penis to hold and perhaps to bite it. A gun is hard and inflexible. The bullets it discharges are also hard as well as penetrating. A gun packs a lot of power, and can be discharged repeatedly without losing any of its force. Since there is reason to believe that slang expressions were originated primarily by men, it is not surprising that they should regard the vagina as a trap, and their own organ as a gun. If one can make contact from a distance by firing a gun, there is no danger of being trapped. Among the Yir Yoront, a primitive Australian tribe who do not have guns, men dream of achieving sexual intercourse by stretching the penis a long distance and penetrating the female.

Slang expressions drawn from the world of nature are much more frequent for the female organs than for the male. The pudendum has been likened to a garden, a flower, an orchard, a rose, and a parsley bed. The only nature reference for the penis is pear. In dreams, there are about as many nature symbols for the male genitals as for the female. Among the common phallic ones are banana and tree. A young man dreamed he was climbing a tree and awoke having an orgasm. Some of the nature metaphors for the female genitals are also found in the list of dream symbols, for example, orchard, flower, and rose.

The use of figures of speech drawn from nature to describe the female body is commonplace in poetry. One of the most beautiful examples is a passage from Shakespeare's *Venus and Adonis* in which Venus is trying to inflame Adonis. She likens her body to a park and "thou shalt be my deer"

Feed where thou wilt, on mountain or in dale;
Graze on my lips; and if those hills be dry,
Stray lower, where the pleasant fountains lie.
Within this limit is relief enough,
Sweet bottom-grass, and high delightful plain,
Round rising hillocks, brakes obscure and rough,
To shelter thee from tempest and from rain.

Scenery in dreams often seems to represent aspects of the human body. Here are a few examples.

I was walking across rolling fields covered with short, fine grass and thrown into swells and hollows of the most graceful contour. Wandering over the green slopes I approached an opening, a great funnel slanting down. I went in. Presently the passage tapered until I could squeeze no further.

I was in the country on a raised plot of ground under the shade of a small spreading tree. I could see my silhouette against the setting sun. The tree was in bloom with white blossoms, the ground had short, green grass, and the countryside was made up of low rolling hills dotted with small white silvery fingers.

Slang expressions and dream symbols for sexual intercourse also have many parallels. The three most common classes of metaphors both in slang and in dreams are: (1) words or images that have an aggressive connotation, such as stab, invade, impale, prod, and poke; (2) words and images describing a mechanical action, such as mounting, penetrating, joining, and thrusting; and (3) words or images which refer to the purely physical work that is involved, as exemplified by the expressions "grinding one's tool," "greasing a wheel," and "climbing a ladder or stairs." The reader will recall the young man who dreamed of inserting a dipstick into the oil reservoir and likened it to intercourse. A man dreamed he was climbing a long flight of stairs and when he reached the top he saw a couple having intercourse.

One of the most common American slang words for coitus is screwing. The analogy between inserting a screw to unite two things and inserting the penis in the vagina to unite two bodies is transparent. Mechanics differentiate between a male screw and a female screw. The male screw is a grooved, cylindrical piece of metal; the female screw is a hollow casting in which the male screw fits.

There is also an etymological basis for the association between screwing and sexual intercourse. The English word *screw* is derived by way of the French from the Latin *scrofa*, which means a female pig. Scrofa was influenced by another Latin word which refers to the vulva. The English word *scrofulous,* which means morally corrupt and degenerate, is derived from the same Latin source as the word screw.

The study of the relation of slang to dream symbols suggests that the metaphorical images of dreams and the metaphorical meaning of words *reveal* our thoughts and feelings rather than conceal them. One astonishing difference between a slang expression and its counterpart in dreams is that we usually know what we are referring to when we use a slang word, but often we have no idea what the referent is when a metaphorical symbol appears in dreams. In fact, we do not even recognize it to be a metaphor. This happens in life, too. So many of the common objects which we use daily, and many words as well, are unrecognized metaphors.

The evidence presented in this chapter indicates that the language we speak, the slang we improvise, the things we invent, live with, and use in our daily life, and the activities we engage in are, whether we know it or not, just as metaphorical as the dreams we have at night. We live in a world of symbols, awake or asleep. Reality and dream are not as day and night; they are both metaphorical and fantastical to the same degree. They both have their roots in and draw their sustenance from the same wishes and fears.

From early childhood, whether in dreams or in waking life, the individual is impelled to gratify his wishes and to banish his fears. He wants mother but he is afraid of losing her or of being punished, emasculated, or killed by father. He wants to return to the womb but he is afraid of suffocation and other dangers. He wants bodily pleasure but he is afraid of retribution. He wants to succeed but he is afraid of failure. He wants freedom but he is afraid of insecurity. He wants to live but he is afraid of dying.

Whether one writes a poem, renovates a house, plays chess, drives a sports car, seeks political office, manages a business, operates a crane, or gambles—in reality or in a dream—he is acting out metaphorically wishes and fears that originated in childhood or in prenatal life or by evolution.

Several centuries ago, the English philosopher John Locke proposed that the mind at birth was a clean slate (*tabula rasa*) upon which the pencil of experience wrote. Our entire mental life, he maintained, is a product of our experiences and owes nothing to inborn traits. Man lives in houses, rides in automobiles, and works in offices or factories because there are houses, automobiles, offices, and factories in his environment. He dreams about them for the same reason; they are there to be dreamed about.

This is a viewpoint that many people prefer because it places the responsibility for their behavior outside of themselves. If a misfortune occurs or if they misbehave, it is not their fault. They are the victims of circumstance. We think it is a simple-minded explanation because it is based on the absurdity that the things in the environment—house, automobiles, offices, and factories—invented themselves.

We hold a *tabula rasa* view, too, but it is a *tabula rasa* of the environment and not of the mind. The environment is the clean slate upon which the mind's ideas, feelings, and fantasies write themselves. At birth, a baby whose mind is filled with fantasies or archetypes enters an *empty* world. Out of his fantasies he fills this empty world with faucets, fountains, hoses, and sprinklers; with tricycles, bicycles, motorcycles, automobiles, and airplanes; with trees, mountains, rivers, and waterfalls; with huts, cabins, houses, and castles; with cigars, ice cream cones, all-day suckers, and lipsticks; with knives, guns, cannons, and bombs; and with cemeteries, headstones, coffins, and wreaths. He invents the whole wide world out of his infantile and archetypal fantasies.

Thanks to the acted-out fantasies of generations of mankind, the world is well-stocked with material metaphors. Psychologically, however, the world is as empty for a baby born today as it was for Adam. The baby's fantasies have to *find* their objects in the world or invent them. Adam entered a world filled with things—trees, stones, waterfalls, caves, and a lovely garden—but he had to find them. They did not go looking for him. They were indifferent. They still are. Man makes his world; the world does not make man.

This does not mean that man sits down and reasons out the sort of world he wants and then goes about creating it. If he did he might have a better world—or a worse one. Whatever planning he does is at the service of wishes and fears of which he is often unaware. It is possible that as our knowledge of human nature increases we will be able to plan a world in which we can live more satisfying lives. This seems dubious, however, since there is little evidence that advances in science and technology have made the world a better place in which to live. Quite the contrary, many people might say.

It might be thought that sufficient objects have been invented to satisfy all the fantasies that man has or possibly could have. Why does he need more and more things? Why doesn't he enjoy what he has? Because he is never satisfied with what is already there. He wants something better than his father had, who in turn wanted something better than *his* father had. Man tames the horse, but that does not satisfy his desire for power. He invents the automobile which is an improvement over the horse. He makes the automobile more and more powerful but it cannot fly. So he dreams an Icarian dream, and out of the dream comes the airplane, the jet, the rocket, the satellite, the spaceship, and so on *ad infinitum*. A desire to outdo one's ancestors is the spur of progress.

Man also looks for symbols that will gratify several wishes at the same time. An automobile is not only a sex symbol but it is a womb symbol and a symbol of aggression as well. A faucet is not only a phallic symbol but it stands for the mother's breast also.

Poetry, fiction, music, and works of art are valued because they sublimate the wishes and fears of mankind. Art and literature are complex and complicated metaphors. That is why they can be endlessly interpreted by critics and analysts.

In summary, our view is that man's waking behavior is just as metaphorical as his dreams are. In waking life, he acts out the same wishes and fears that determine the contents of his dreams. For this reason the study of dreams can help us understand why we live as we do. Dreams reveal what lies behind the looking glass of everyday life.

Chapter 8

A Point of View

It is not our intention in this chapter to formulate a theory of dreams. There is simply not enough tested knowledge upon which to support a comprehensive theory. Furthermore, the formulation of a theory inevitably creates barriers which exclude new ideas, stifles innovative thinking, and produces a tradition which is resistant to change. We believe a theory that is stated prematurely is more harmful than beneficial.

Our intention in this chapter is to present a point of view that has evolved from our studies of dreams and that remains relatively close to the findings of these studies. We will speculate on what the results of our investigations mean regarding the nature of man and the kind of environment and society that he has devised to live in. To speculate means to play with ideas in order to stimulate new thinking and new investigations that may advance our knowledge of dreams and human nature. It is not our intention to be dogmatic, inflexible, or finalistic about what we have to say.

The cornerstone of our viewpoint is the Aristotelian dictum that dreaming is thinking during sleep. There are, we feel, no important differences between what we think about while we are awake and what we dream about while we are asleep. The motives that energize and direct the course of thinking and that provide the substance of our thoughts are the same motives that energize and direct the course of dreaming and that provide the contents of dreams. We believe these motives are wishes and fears that develop during childhood and that may have their roots in prenatal experiences and racial history. Wishes and fears do not change after childhood, although the ways in which they express themselves through thought and action may and *do* change.

If dreaming is simply a continuation of waking mental activity, why would it not be simpler to collect and analyze daytime thoughts instead of dreams? Collecting daytime thoughts presents a number of difficulties. If a person is asked to report what he is thinking, the task of self-observation itself becomes the mental activity. It is difficult, if not impossible, for a person to stand on the sidelines as an observer and describe what is passing through his mind. The mind cannot observe and be observed at the same time. To complicate the task, the person must describe in words what he is observing while he is continuing to observe it. Thinking is such a rapid process that it is impossible for the observer, who is also the transcriber, to keep up the pace. Furthermore, since we do not ordinarily think in words but in some abbreviated form, it is very difficult to translate thoughts into language at the necessary speed. A large part of our thinking is carried on at a level below that of conscious awareness and is inaccessible for observation.

It is true that we can usually say in a general way what we have been thinking about. "I was thinking about making out my income tax." "I was thinking about the book I was going to write." "I was thinking about painting the bedroom." Such reports lack the vital details so necessary for analysis.

Often we are reticent to describe our thoughts, so we remain silent or censor them. A person is not likely to admit that he was thinking about murdering his spouse or having sex with his daughter or wrecking his father's car or torturing his neighbor, even if such thoughts *did* enter his mind. Many of them never reach the level of consciousness.

None of these impediments applies to dreams. A dream is a succession of images, usually visual, which, when remembered, can be as easily described in words as a motion picture we saw last night.

Dreams objectify that which is subjective, they visualize that which is invisible, they transform the abstract into the concrete, and they make conscious that which is unconscious. They come from the most archaic alcoves of the mind as well as from the peripheral levels of waking consciousness. Dreams are the kaleidoscope of the mind.

The dreamer is both subject and object. As subject, he witnesses the dream in the same way that a spectator witnesses a play. As object, he is a participant in the dream which he, as subject, is watching. Neither of these roles changes the course of the action. Nor is the dream greatly influenced by external events; it is essentially an autonomous mental activity. Since we do not feel responsible for our dreams, we are less likely to conceal or censor them than we are our waking thoughts.

For all of these reasons, dreams are of great value to the psychologist and anyone else who wishes to study the contents of the mind in their most observable and revealed manifestations.

One does not dream, however, in order to provide psychologists with information about the mind or about human nature. Nor do we have dreams in order to recall them in the morning, to tell them to our friends, or to our psychoanalyst. They are not messages or omens or prophecies; they are not the experiences of a disembodied soul; they are not the movements of the eyeballs; they are not the guardians or sentinels of sleep; and they do not reduce tension by fulfilling wishes. They exist for their own reasons, whatever those reasons may be. (We suspect the reasons reside in the nature of the brain.) But because they do exist we can utilize them advantageously in exploring the contents of the mind.

Although we have said a dream is a sequence of images which are imaginary rather than real, a person is not aware of this distinction while experiencing a dream. He does not see images; he sees people and objects and actions, and he sees himself in their midst. Everything he dreams about is authentic to him. In waking life he would not ordinarily confuse thoughts with perceptions or with actions.

Thinking in waking life usually but not always culminates eventually in some sort of action. Dreaming, as ordinarily defined, always involves imaginary action. We have shown there is continuity between thinking while we are awake, and dreaming while we are asleep.

What then is the relationship between actions in dreams and actions in waking life. If I dream of burning my neighbor's house Wednesday night, I will not necessarily set fire to it on Thursday. I may wait until Friday or next week or next year! What is more likely, I will engage in some displaced or substitute form of action. I may burn leaves close to his back porch on a windy day. I may inadvertently (?) let my sprinkler splash water on his clean windows. I may accidentally (?) drop a burning cigarette on his carpet or spill beer on his table. I may borrow a match or try to sell him additional fire insurance. I may invite him to join a volunteer fire squad. I may loan him James Baldwin's book *The Fire Next Time*. There are innumerable ways in which I can displace the acted-out wish in the dream. Conscience-stricken, I may even burn down my own house—accidentally!

The point is there is no exact correspondence between deeds in dreams and deeds in waking life. There is, however, an exact correspondence between the wishes and fears that are acted out in dreams and the wishes and fears that are acted out in waking life. It is the way in which they are acted out that differs. They are often more directly expressed or more thinly disguised in dreams than they are in waking life. We learn to use all kinds of subterfuges, including rationalization, displacement, sublimation, symbolization, projection, and reaction formation, in waking life to conceal our wishes and fears even from ourselves. Some of these contrivances, especially symbolization, are also used in dreams but to a lesser extent than when we are awake. Dreams may not always be a reliable indication of how a person will act when he is awake, but they can be depended upon to reveal the underlying motivation for his behavior often in a crude yet unmistakable form.

Let us place the question of the relation of dreams to deeds in a larger perspective. We believe that the universal themes in dreams are reflected in group behavior and social institutions to the same extent that they are in individual behavior.

It is generally recognized that among the reasons why men formed groups and created institutions are those of protection and security. Who is man protecting himself from? Supposedly from "acts of God," "alien enemies," each other, and in the case of people living close to nature, from wild animals. This is self-evident. What is not so obvious or acceptable as an explanation is that a social organization protects a person from his own impulses.

Consider, for instance, one feature of a society; its legal system with its paraphernalia of laws, policemen, courts, judges, and penal institutions. A legal system serves the purpose not only of discouraging my neighbor from burning my house but also of discouraging me from burning his house. The law protects both of us by threatening to punish each of us equally for committing the same illegal act. It protects me from my neighbor's destructive impulses, but it also protects me from suffering the painful consequences of expressing *my* destructive impulses. But since his aggression and mine are both curbed by fear of punishment, it appears that the main purpose of a legal system is to protect a person from his own impulses. If the system does its job well, then there are few house-burnings and other impulsive acts, but there is a lot of repressed hostility that must find other outlets, including self-destructive acts.

Actually, a legal system is probably not necessary for most people. Their destructive impulses are effectively restrained by their consciences. Those with undeveloped or weak consciences need external restraints, but even these restraints, as the crime statistics tell us, are not conspicuously effective.

There are at least two unfortunate consequences that result from establishing social institutions to curb impulses. Social institutions are operated by people who have aggressive impulses themselves. The nature of their work permits them to express their aggression directly against the "enemies of society." Thus, it should not surprise anyone that policemen or prison guards are often overzealous in the performance of their duties, since they can "get away with it." Not only do they find outlets for their hostility but they also may use their positions of authority to gratify their polymorphous sexual impulses.

Moreover, since the administration of justice is in the hands of people who have the same human nature as anyone else, they are exposed to influence from those with more power or more money or more distinction than they have. Thus, it happens that people who break the same law are not always treated equally.

In order to show the relationship between dreams and the legal system, we made a study of dreams that contained references to prisons, policemen, and trials. Most of the dreams were about policemen; few contained references to prisons or trials.

The policeman is a fairly ubiquitous person in dreams, and he plays several roles. Most frequently, he is arresting the dreamer or another character for an illegal act. The offenses range from a traffic violation to murder. Sometimes no offense is committed but the dreamer is arrested anyway. In one such dream, the dreamer was driving with his girl up and down hills on a side road, and was stopped by a policeman and given a citation. In some dreams, the dreamer apprehends criminals and calls the police. In others, the dreamer is in danger or has something stolen, and the police come to his aid. Occasionally, a policeman enacts a friendly role. For example, a dreamer was looking for entertainment and a policeman told him where he could find a gambling place.

Since most of the crimes clearly consist of the expression of aggressive or sexual impulses, the policeman as an arresting or restraining authority represents the externalized superego (conscience). One can say equally well that the superego plays the role of the policeman in the personality. External world and internal personality are symmetrical. (This is one of the most important generalizations that can be made regarding the relationship of dreams and life.)

Even when the dreamer turns criminals over to the police or watches others being arrested, he is actually having his own "criminal" impulses arrested. A man dreamed that the police arrested some young men and imprisoned them in a house. The dreamer was afraid to go in the house, so he looked at them through a window. In several dreams, the criminals simply vanished when the police arrived. A woman dreamed she was about to be raped when the police (conscience) intervened. An interesting variation of this type of dream was reported by another woman. She walked past a police car and thought of the safety it implied. She was then followed by a man and became very frightened. Apparently the protection provided by the police (superego) was not effective enough to prevent her having rape fantasies. In another woman's dream, the dreamer ran home when she was chased by a man, and her mother and brother killed the would-be attacker. They then called the police to remove the dead body.

The friendly policeman represents a friendly conscience, that is, one that sides with the dreamer's impulses rather than opposing them. A man dreamed a policeman took him to his pleasant cottage located in the middle of a deplorable slum area where the dreamer had just been attacked. In the dream, the dreamer felt that the policeman wanted to live with the people he policed, and that he understood and sympathized with them.

This amity between conscience and impulse does not usually work, however. In a dream in which the policeman was friendly, he was reported to his chief by no less an authority than President Truman! In another dream, the dreamer was speeding in a "hot rod" to a racetrack when he was stopped by the police. They obligingly escorted him to the racetrack, but when the dreamer entered a race he lost control of his car and crashed against the fence.

The brutality of the superego is depicted in a dream in which the dreamer watched the police battle a group of strikers. They clubbed the strikers and rode their horses over them.

Trial and prison dreams are mere extensions of these police dreams. The judge or jailer acts toward the dreamer as his conscience does. Confinement in prison reflects restraints imposed upon the impulses by the superego. The dreamer often dreams of trying to break out of jail.

These dreams unveil the psychological meaning of a social institution. They indicate that man has devised a legal system to curb his own impulses. The legal system is the external counterpart of an internal system. Just as "criminals" are impulses, so policemen, judges, and jailers are punitive superegos. Naturally, the penalties fall heaviest on those groups such as Negroes, Indians, and "aliens" who themselves symbolize primitive behavior, whether in dreams or in waking life.

Is the nature of society responsible for what we dream about, or do our dreams determine the nature of society? In our opinion, no causal relation exists between dreams and society, just as no causal relation exists between dreams and thoughts. Dreams and the social order, dreams and actions, and dreams and thoughts, are all expressions of the same basic wishes and fears of mankind. The dynamics of dreams are also the dynamics of society. Consequently, when we study dreams we are not only studying the individual but we are also studying his social behavior and the institutions he creates.

In an earlier chapter, we gave reasons for rejecting the idea that man's behavior is determined by the environment in which he lives. Instead, we advocated the view that man makes his own world. The question can then be asked; what sort of human nature is it that would produce the world of physical objects and the world of social, political, and economic institutions and arrangements that constitute Western civilization? (We are restricting the question to Western civilization not because we think civilizations whether "advanced" or "primitive" are essentially different—we don't —but because we do not wish to get sidetracked by this issue. We will present evidence in another book that "civilizations" are all pretty much alike.)

Why do we have houses, apartments, offices, factories, farms, automobiles, and airplanes? Why do we have games like football, baseball, basketball, tennis, golf, and bowling? Why do we have schools, churches, clubs, museums, prisons, hospitals, bars, cemeteries, and parks? Why do we have marriage and divorce? Why do we have books, magazines, newspapers, radio, television, and movies? Why do we have laws, regulations, and rules? Why do we have shoes, watches, whistles, electric blankets, playing cards, bottles, shovels, and gardens? Why do we have paintings, symphonies, sculptures, poems, and novels? Why have we filled our world with all of these things and many, many more?

An analysis of dreams provides answers to these questions. On a very general level, dreams teach us that we are constantly trying to maximize our pleasures and minimize our fears. The task is never-ending because every increase in pleasure is inevitably accompanied by an increase in anxiety. A person must learn to make compromises between wishes and fears, so that he obtains some enjoyment without arousing too much anxiety. This means that he is never completely satisfied but it also means that he is never overwhelmed by anxiety. All of the things listed above enable us, in some degree, to work out compromises between wishes and fears.

These are generalities. When we come down to individual cases, there are differences in the strength of the wishes and differences in the strength of the fears. One person is more easily satisfied or more fearful than another person. Differences in practical judgment enable one person to find more satisfying compromises than another person. Education expands one's opportunities to discover new and better compromises. So does a culturally rich environment and an open society.

We have presented examples throughout this book of the various kinds of compromises people make. Some have been more successful than others.

There was the middle-aged man who wanted to be a woman. Either the desire was not strong enough, or the fear was stronger, to make him undergo a medical and surgical transformation, as others have done. Nor was it strong enough to overcome his reluctance to join the underground world of transvestism. He was not sufficiently oriented toward homosexuality to make that way of life attractive to him, although his dreams revealed a strong impulse to have sexual relations with males. He may also have been afraid of the consequences of openly gratifying his desire to be either a woman or a homosexual.

Instead, he found what was for him a satisfying solution. During the day he was a man, and at night, in the privacy of his home, he was a woman. He married, whether by design or by good fortune, a woman who accepted his transvestism and who even taught him how to be more womanlike in dress, grooming, and expressive behavior. Their sex life was satisfactory, he was the father of two daughters, and he and his wife seemed to be happy together.

At times, he may have wanted something more—to have homosexual relations, for example—but he had enough practical judgment to foresee the possible dangers and dissatisfactions of indulging himself. This does not mean that he is permanently immune to his cravings. Were these cravings to grow in strength or were the internal barriers to weaken, practical judgment might no longer be effective. Then he might find himself in trouble. Or it might motivate him to find an even better kind of life. One is either on the brink of disaster or on the threshold of a new discovery.

The child molester, also a middle-aged man, was not so fortunate. His impulses to investigate the genitals of children occasionally overcame his fear of the consequences, and resulted in severe problems for him. Most of the time, however, he was able to control himself by staying home with his mother and sister, and by avoiding outside associations. More satisfying compromises were available to him but he had not yet discovered them.

Another one of our dreamers who was attracted to youths of both sexes had found a somewhat satisfying arrangement by becoming a teacher in a junior high school. He had some sexual outlets with his pupils, but he handled them with sufficient discretion so he avoided trouble except once when he was questioned by the police. There is no guarantee that he will continue to stay out of trouble. He has chosen a rather dangerous course.

Franz Kafka's aversion to his own body caused him to abuse it so extensively that he contracted tuberculosis and died.

The Bostonian who dreamed so frequently of physiological

processes, especially elimination, found a happy solution by becoming a physiology teacher. He could indulge his interests in the internal workings of the body and his body destruction fantasies by choosing a profession which sanctioned such interests.

One of our dream correspondents found outlets for her wishes and fears in writing, and another by becoming a psychologist.

The engineer who has been sending us his dreams for several years is still struggling to find a way of life that will free him from the bonds of love and hate which bind him to his father and mother. He and his wife are now divorced but this is not likely to solve anything as long as the original parental ties are still intact. He is thinking of becoming a psychologist, which is a method of intellectualizing his conflicts. It remains to be seen whether this will be successful.

The adolescent who kept a dream diary from age 15 to age 19 has since become an adult. After several years of serious conflict and tension, he seems to be experiencing a more harmonious relationship with his environment. Instead of fighting or denying his impulses, he now accepts them and is searching for realistic ways of discharging them.

The value to the individual of keeping a dream diary is that it provides him with an objective record of *his* specific conflicts and concerns. It is these conflicts and these concerns that he has to confront and resolve if he is to find some degree of contentment in his life. They cannot be evaded or discarded. They will not go away of their own accord, and they will not be outgrown. One simply cannot blot out one's heredity, one's prenatal existence, or one's childhood.

Compromise is rarely a permanent solution. As wishes and fears ebb and flow they require new adjustments. One never knows when an old enemy will appear at the door. As dreams show us, there is an endless repetition of aggressions, punishments, polymorphous sexual cravings, fears and anxieties, guilt feelings and frustrations. They are always on the threshold of one's life, waiting to gain entry. Against them no locks or fastenings can be permanently effective.

Freud taught us that the wishes and fears which develop during childhood (their roots may lie in heredity and in prenatal existence) are timeless. They never change and they never perish. This is confirmed by dreams. The same themes of sex and sadism, separation anxiety and sibling rivalry, body destruction and castration anxiety, ambivalence and bisexuality, love and hate, guilt and remorse, and frustration and failure keep reappearing year in and year out. If they are in dreams they must be, according to the continuity hypothesis, in our waking life, too.

Superimposed upon this basic edifice of wishes and fears in waking life is an intricate scaffolding of displacements, symbolizations, intellectualizations, sublimations, reaction formations, denials, and projections which conceals the structure it encloses. In dreams, much though not all of this scaffolding is removed, so that the underlying structure can be more easily seen. Once the wishes and fears are disclosed we can return to waking life and begin to apprehend the reasons for the scaffolding. It protects us—usually very poorly—from our wishes and fears.

We can ask ourselves whether some of the scaffolding is useless and can be removed or simplified without harm to ourselves. We can ask ourselves whether the present scaffolding might not be replaced with better material which will permit us to live more satisfying or less desperate lives. At the same time we should also ask the painful question: What kind of world is possible, given the nature of man's dreams as described in this book? Can a better world be fashioned by men who have bad dreams?

Our point of view, briefly stated, is that the truth revealed in dreams is the same truth we have to face and deal with in waking life. How we deal with that truth while we are asleep and dreaming is not in itself important. How we deal with it during waking life is of the greatest importance to our personal well-being and to the well-being of society.

Chapter 9

How to Analyze
Your Own Dreams

The following guide is written for people who would like to analyze their own dreams. The methods of analysis described here do not require a background of specialized knowledge or technical information. In fact, it is preferable if a person is not too familiar with dream theories so that he can approach the study of his dreams with an open, receptive, unprejudiced mind. We suggest to the reader that he adopt the attitude of "reading *out*" of his dreams what is in them instead of "reading *into*" his dreams what he has learned from books.

The methods set forth here are easy to learn and use. The principal qualifications to be a good dream analyst are good judgment, careful attention to detail, patience—and courage. Patience is a basic requirement for two reasons. The methods, though easy to learn, require a lot of sustained effort classifying, counting, and compiling in order to discover the valuable information that dreams can provide when they are thoroughly analyzed. Patience is also necessary because one has to keep a written record of his dreams for several months before the analysis can begin.

We mention courage as a necessary qualification because it takes fortitude to admit to oneself some of the implications that are suggested by the analysis of dreams. Dreams often depict feelings that we prefer to keep hidden even from ourselves, and that we often rationalize away in waking life. Dreams are not very considerate of the conscious image we have of ourselves. One of their great merits is that they are completely honest. Self-deception, which is all too common in waking life, does not exist in dreams. One should be on guard against letting his conscious self-image prejudice the interpretation of dreams.

Why should a person be interested in analyzing his dreams? The best reason, we believe, is to increase self-knowledge. Dreams are an invaluable source of information about the feelings and thoughts of the dreamer. Feelings and thoughts are, by their very nature, subjective. Not only is it difficult for a person to appraise and understand the feelings and thoughts of another person, but it is also difficult to describe his own feelings and thoughts. Dreams objectify the dreamer's feelings and thoughts. They do this by visualizing the inner mental states which ordinarily remain abstract or invisible. The dreamer can see what he is thinking and feeling.

This guide does not attempt to tell the reader what his dreams mean. It does not present fixed interpretations of specific dreams or dream elements. It does not translate the symbols of dreams into their referents. It is not a "dream book" in the usual sense.

Although there are common dreams that everyone has, and that may have universal meanings, most dreams are personal in character. No two persons have the same pattern of dreams. This is why ordinary dream books are not suitable for interpreting dreams, and may even be misleading.

This guide describes methods for analyzing dreams and suggests how the results of the analysis may be used to interpret dreams in order to enhance self-understanding. Examples of what particular types of dreams or dream elements may mean are given solely for the purpose of stimulating thought. They suggest what one might look for in interpreting dreams but in no case are these interpretations to be accepted uncritically as the correct meanings. For example, the suggestion is made that dreams in which the dreamer suffers a misfortune represent self-punishment. This interpretation makes a lot of sense and is probably valid for many such dreams. But you must be on the alert for other possible meanings as well. In another place, the suggestion is made that scenery in dreams—rolling hills, mountains, valleys, forests, rivers, lakes, and waterfalls—represent the dreamer's body or another person's body. This suggestion may prove to be useful for understanding some dreams but it would be a mistake to impress this meaning upon all scenic dreams. In other words, consider the suggestions we make but also consider other possible meanings. One's understanding of dreams, and through them of himself, will be greatly enhanced by maintaining an open, inquiring attitude. Ideas that the dreamer encounters in his reading about dreams can be tried out on his own dreams to see whether they fit or not.

The essential feature of our method of analyzing dreams is that one analyzes a series of dreams and not single dreams. A single dream reflects only one vista of the mind. A series of dreams reveals the whole panorama of the mind. Before discussing methods of analyzing dreams, we must first discuss how to go about collecting a series of dreams.

Collecting Dreams

The methods of dream analysis described in this guide require one to collect at least one hundred of his dreams before beginning an analysis. This is the most arduous step of the entire project. A person may be strongly motivated when he begins his dream diary but will soon discover it is a demanding task which requires considerable self-discipline. By establishing a routine the task will become habitual and will seem just as natural as performing other daily routines. When this is achieved, recording one's dreams will be self-sustaining, making it as difficult a habit to break as it was to establish.

Recalling dreams

One method of keeping a dream diary is to have a pad and pencil beside the bed to make notes on dreams during the night. The dream can then be reconstructed from these notes the next day. Or if one wants to describe the dream completely when awakening during the night, he may use a tape recorder to do so. He then must transcribe the dream to paper in order to analyze it. Neither of these methods is essential, however. If one is too meticulous about recalling his dreams he is likely to lose interest.

We prefer a more relaxed, natural method. After awakening, spend a few minutes searching your memory for dreams. If none can be recalled do not pursue the matter. Do not become anxious; there will be other nights which produce dreams you can recall.

During the night when you recall a dream, review it in your mind before returning to sleep. Then in the morning you can type or write the dream, making it a part of your permanent dream record. Reviewing the dream during the night proves very effective for vivid recall in the morning. Many of the less dramatic dreams would be otherwise forgotten.

Sometimes dreams that cannot be recalled in the morning are recalled later in the day. These dreams should also be recorded in your dream diary.

Format

You should record your dreams on 5″ by 8″ index cards, which are obtainable at any stationery store. Each dream should be written or typed on a separate card. If two or more dreams are recalled from one night, *each dream should be recorded on a separate card.* The reason we suggest 5″ by 8″ cards is that they are durable, easy to file, and easy to handle during the actual analysis.

On the top right corner of the card record the date the dream occurred. On the top left corner of the card number the dreams consecutively. If two or more dreams are recalled from one night, they should be numbered in the order in which they were dreamed, if that distinction is possible.

People often recall dreams after taking a nap. If a nap dream is recalled, it should be dated and numbered on a card the same as a night dream.

What is a dream?

Anything that a person experiences while he is asleep and recalls when he awakes is considered to be a dream. A dream is ordinarily a sequence of images, ideas, and emotions, appearing in any combination. We think of all dreams as possessing imagery, although occasionally a dream will be devoid of any images whatsoever. It may only be a brief emotion or an abstract idea. Reveries (daydreams) before going to sleep or shortly after waking are not dreams. Some dreams are extremely brief, only a single image, or they can be lengthy and complex. Regardless of length, whether five words or five hundred, we urge you to record *all* dreams.

A person may decide to omit certain dreams from the record, either because he feels they are unimportant or because they are too distasteful to put down in writing. By evaluating or selecting dreams before entering them in the dream record, your final analysis is certain to be erroneous. In order to obtain the most accurate results from your dream research you must record *every* dream.

Sometimes it may be difficult to decide whether a long dream in which scenes and events shift is one continuous dream or if it is two or more separate dreams. You will have to decide this yourself since there is no objective rule to follow. Ordinarily you can detect whether it is a single dream or several dreams.

Describing a dream

When writing the description of a dream be as accurate and objective as possible. The description should portray exactly in words what one has dreamed in pictures, no more and no less. The manner used to describe a dream is similar to describing a play or movie.

One precautionary measure should be emphasized. *In your dream description never attempt to clarify the dream.* Some dreams are recalled in a rather chaotic manner, so one is tempted to revise the dream, making it more coherent. The reason this should never be done is that the revised version will change the actual dream content. If the dream is disjointed, chaotic, or bizarre, leave it this way when you record it. This then is the true dream.

A typical dream consists of one or more settings, one or more characters or animals besides the dreamer, interactions between the characters and the dreamer, various objects and activities, and emotions. It is like watching a play except that the dreamer is a participant as well as a spectator. (Rarely is the dreamer only a spectator.) In any event, the details of this nocturnal drama, as they are recalled, should be accurately described when recording the dream.

If certain aspects of the dream are unclear or forgotten, substitutes should not be inserted. If one of the dream characters cannot be recalled for certain, this should be so designated rather than supplying a probable name. If a character appears to be either A or B, you should indicate this rather than arbitrarily deciding on A rather than B. This rule applies to all features of the dream. If there is confusion or uncertainty in recalling the dream, this is the way it should appear in the dream report.

The basic rule is: *Don't omit anything that can be recalled and don't add anything that cannot be recalled.*

Avoid any tendency to write a prolific essay or literary masterpiece when describing a dream. You should concentrate on clear expository writing, with your attention on the dream and not on the style of writing.

Additional information

After the dream has been accurately described, the dreamer may wish to note some observations or information he feels may be pertinent to the dream. For example, he may awaken during the night remembering a dream and observe he was lying in a cramped position, or was cold, or had to go to the bathroom. Or he may be faintly aware of hearing a siren, a bell ringing, or a door slamming. Any physical condition or external stimulation may be noted on the dream card if the dreamer feels it influenced his dream.

Events of the previous day or of the more remote past which seem to be represented in the dream may also be noted. These may be public events or personal experiences. The dream may also be influenced by reading material, movies, television programs, social events, or people one has seen recently.

There are two other items of information that may be noted on the dream record. One is the presence of color. In many dreams the dreamer is not aware of any color whatsoever, while other dreams appear to be entirely in color, like a Technicolor movie. More frequently, though, the dreamer recalls specific objects as being colored, such as a red car or a blue dress. Whatever the case may be—no color, some color, or all color—this should be noted on the card, since it is a part of the dream experience.

The dreamer should also record the emotion associated with the dream. It may be a very enjoyable or a terribly frightening dream. The same dream may contain pleasant and unpleasant experiences. Or it may be a neutral dream which arouses no emotion. The dreamer may experience anger, fear, grief, amusement, pleasure, frustration, or confusion. We experience the same emotions in dreams as we do in waking life, sometimes much more intensely. You should try to assess the exact emotion experienced while the dream took place and note it on the dream card.

You should not become too involved in explaining or interpreting any particular dream during the time it is being recorded. This could become burdensome and retard one's interest in the project. The *notes* are not essential for dream analysis. The actual dream content is what is essential, and will disclose its meaningfulness when a large number of dreams has been collected. For example, you might have a dream in which you are skiing on the Swiss Alps. In waking life you have never skiied and have never been in Switzerland, but the night before the dream you watched a Swiss travelogue film. In your notes, then, you could indicate that this dream occurred after watching a Swiss movie. This notation would be nonessential in the dream analysis but might be useful in other connections, as we will point out later.

Aids to recalling dreams

Many people cannot remember their dreams, and some believe that they never dream at all. The latter statement is incorrect. Everyone dreams every night throughout his entire life. The brain continues its function during sleep the same as the heart and lungs continue their functions during sleep.

It is true, however, that people differ greatly in their ability to recall dreams. There are a few people that have never recalled a dream, and they know about dreams only by reading or through conversation. Most people remember an occasional dream, maybe one every couple of days. Then there are a small number of people who can remember one or more dreams every night. It is not known with certainty why there should be these differences among people in recalling dreams.

How can one improve his memory for dreams? Most important is one's attitude. If a person becomes sufficiently interested in dreams and pays attention to them, his recall will improve automatically. There will not be instant improvement, however; you must sustain interest long enough before obtaining results. Even after you begin recalling dreams on a regular basis, there will be periods when no dreams can be recalled. These barren periods will pass and return, as unpredictably as the weather.

Various devices that may help dream recall have already been mentioned, such as having tape recorder or pad and pencil accessible during the night. Another method is self-suggestion, or conditioning yourself before going to sleep that you will remember your dreams. When first awakening in the morning, think immediately what has been going on in your mind during sleep. Do this before planning any daily activities, conducting any business, or whatever. It is a very simple procedure, but something few people have ever tried. We are so preoccupied with our waking-hour activities that we really haven't given our night-hour activities much thought. We hope to show in this book that paying attention to one's dreams can be immensely rewarding.

If you share a bedroom with another person, you can relate your dreams to him. This would be another incentive for remembering dreams. A family may wish to recount their dreams at the breakfast table. Not only will this socialize the remembering of dreams but it will also inculcate habits of recalling dreams in children. Even very young children can remember their dreams.

If all else fails, one can set an alarm two or three times during the night, and try to recall a dream when awakened. This method is not very convenient, but it does work as a last resort.

Some or all the foregoing stratagems may be employed for remembering dreams but a *genuine, sustained interest in one's dreams is the best reason for remembering them.*

Now that you have a collection of dreams, we will describe methods for extracting meaning from them.

Content Analysis: Characters and Interactions with Them

The purpose of analyzing dreams, as stated previously, is to increase self-understanding. Dreams reveal things about us that cannot be readily found from other sources. Moreover, they usually portray our true feelings, in contrast to the self-deceptions, either conscious or unconscious, that we practice in waking life. It is ironical that we must close our eyes in sleep in order to open our eyes about our real feelings. Sleep is oblivious to the social conventions that do so much to encourage self-deception and hypocrisy.

Often there is a split between our feelings toward people in waking life and our behavior toward them. We feel one way and act in an opposite way. In dreams, we act out our true feelings. We do in dreams what we dare not do in waking life. It is sometimes said that dreams are disguises, whereas in actuality it is waking life that is apt to be the disguise.

As explained in Chapter 3, the method we employ for analyzing dreams is known as content analysis. Content analysis consists of extracting the elements that constitute a dream, classifying the elements, and counting the occurrence of each element. By combining similar elements that occur throughout a series of dreams, one obtains an overall picture of the dreamer's preoccupations, feelings, thoughts, problems, and conflicts.

There are many elements in a dream. A dream usually has a *locale* or *setting;* it takes place in a house, at the seashore, or on a street. Various *objects* are recognized. *People* and *animals* appear and often the dreamer *interacts* with them. *Activities* are engaged in and *emotions* are felt. The experiences in dreams contain all of the elements of waking life, plus many others. Classifying these elements and counting the number of times that each element or class of elements occurs in a series of dreams is the primary task of content analysis. From the resulting figures one can then draw some conclusions or inferences.

How do you begin to make a content analysis of a dream series? We prefer to start the analysis by listing the people and animals that appear in a series of dreams, and the kinds of interactions that the dreamer has with these human and animal characters.

Characters

The first step is to list the characters, both human and animal, that appear in Dream 1, Dream 2, Dream 3, and so on throughout the one hundred dreams. There will be several hundred characters in this list. Not all of them will be different people, because the same person may appear in a number of dreams. Regardless of how many dreams a specific person appears in, he should always be listed for each dream. But if he makes several appearances in the same dream he should only be listed once for that dream.

As each character is identified, the kinds of interaction that the dreamer has with that character should be noted.

These two operations, listing the characters and describing the dreamer's interactions with them, will be explained in detail.

What is a character?

A character is any person or animal that the dreamer perceives or thinks about while he is dreaming. Usually, he is seen, but sometimes he is only heard, as when the dreamer is talking with him by telephone. He may not even appear in the dream. The dreamer may receive a letter from him, see him on television or in a movie, read about him in the newspaper, or merely think about him.

Identifying the characters

Some of the characters will be known by name to the dreamer. These are members of his family, relatives, friends and acquaintances, prominent persons, fictitious characters, and some supernatural beings. (We will leave aside animals for a moment.) Some persons may be familiar to the dreamer without his knowing their names—a postman, policeman, or store clerk, for example.

Then there are those characters whom the dreamer does not recognize. These unidentifiable persons (strangers) often have some identifiable characteristic. They are either men or women, or boys or girls. They may be babies. In addition to sex and age, their race or nationality or vocation or status in society may be recognized. Occasionally, nothing is known about the character, not even his sex. Such a person is listed as "someone."

There are also groups of people who act as a unit and cannot be differentiated. The dreamer may see a group of people or a crowd. The group may consist of men, or women, or children, or a mixture of these. They may be soldiers, policemen, a football team, an orchestra, or Orientals. Groups should be identified as clearly as possible.

Animals

Animals are not uncommon elements in dreams, and appear very frequently in dreams reported by children. Animals should be listed as they appear in a dream series, and identified by species, if that is possible. If the animal is one that is known to the dreamer, that should be noted. Groups of animals may also appear in dreams.

Other considerations

Corpses are recorded as characters. When a person changes into another person in the course of a dream, both persons should be listed. If the dreamer cannot decide whether it was one person or another—for example, his wife or his mother—he should say so, but not list them separately. If the same person makes several appearances *in the same dream,* he is to be listed only once.

A sample list of characters

DREAM 1

Mother
Father
Joe (brother)
Aunt Mildred
Cousin Jane
Dog (Rover)

DREAM 2

Mr. Roberts (teacher)
Students (known males and females)
Teacher (male stranger)
Football team (known males)
Referee (stranger)
Band (male and female strangers)

DREAM 3

Jim (friend)
Joan (friend)
Sharks
Sailors (male strangers)
Someone
Dead man

DREAM 4

Mary (friend)
Policeman (stranger)
Horse
Crowd
Minister (stranger)
President Nixon

DREAM 5

Women (known)
Mrs. Smith (acquaintance)
Nurse (female stranger)
Doctor (male stranger)
Grandfather Jones
Mother-in-law
Old lady (stranger)

DREAM 6

Jesus
Abraham Lincoln
Hamlet
Witch

DREAM 7

No characters except for dreamer

DREAM 8

People (male and female)
Burglars (males)
Snake
Tramp (male)
Baby (sex not known)
Children (male and female)
Dorothy (acquaintance)

The dreamer who is analyzing his own dreams will know who the various named and known characters are and need not include the information we have placed within parentheses.

Interactions

Four principal types of interactions between the dreamer and the characters in his dreams take place. These are: (1) aggression, (2) friendliness; (3) sex; and (4) neutral. With some characters, there will be no interactions; they merely appear in the dream.

Aggression

Aggression includes murder, physical assault, chasing, arrest, detention, coercion, destructiveness, stealing, reprimands, threats, criticism, name-calling, quarreling, sneers, and so forth. It also includes feelings of anger, irritation, annoyance, and antagonism.

For each character with whom the dreamer has an aggressive interaction, the kind of aggression should be noted. Also to be noted is whether the dreamer or the character takes the initiative in starting the aggression.

If the aggressive interaction consists of a sequence of different kinds of aggression with a character, only the most serious one of the sequence need be recorded. For example, if a quarrel ends in a physical fight, the fight alone is recorded.

Friendliness

Friendliness includes having a good time with a person (aside from frankly sexual activities), doing a favor, giving a present, visiting, inviting, becoming engaged or married, making friendly remarks, greetings, compliments, physical expressions of friendliness such as shaking hands and kissing (nonsexual), and feeling friendly, grateful, or sympathetic.

Friendly interactions should be identified in the same way that aggressive ones are.

Sex

All forms of interactions that the dreamer regards as being sexual in character should be recorded. These fall under the general heading of "making love." Also to be included are sexual feelings.

The dreamer may interact with the same character in the same dream in more than one way. He may be both sexual and hostile, for example. Both kinds of interactions should be recorded.

Neutral

Some interactions are not accompanied by any feeling tone. The dreamer merely interacts with another character in a matter-of-fact, neutral way. Examples of such interactions are conversing, making a purchase, watching an athletic event or dramatic performance, playing a game, looking at someone, and so forth. It is not necessary to describe the type of neutral interaction. Merely indicate that it is neutral. If the dreamer has both a neutral and either an aggressive, friendly, or sexual encounter with the same character in a dream, the neutral interaction is *not* recorded.

The Record Sheet

The record sheet on which the foregoing entries are to be made consists of six columns. The number of the dream should be placed in the first column. Characters (other than the dreamer) appearing in each dream are listed in the second column. The other four columns are for the four types of interactions. This is an example of how the record sheet should look. D is the abbreviation for the dreamer.

DREAM	CHARACTERS	AGGRESSION	FRIEND-LINESS	SEX	NEUTRAL
1	Mother		D does favor for		
	Father	D quarrels with			
	Joe	Reprimands D			
	Aunt Mildred				
	Cousin Jane	Criticizes D	D kisses her		neutral
	Dog	Barks at D	D pets him		
2	Mr. Roberts				neutral
	Students				neutral
	Teacher	Accuses D of cheating			
	Football team				neutral
	Referee		Compliments D		
	Band				neutral
3	Jim		D shakes hands with		
	Joan			Embraces	
	Sharks	Chase D			
	Sailors		Rescue D		
	Someone	Steals D's clothes			
	Dead man				neutral
4	Mary			Sexual inter-course	
	Policeman	Arrests D			
	Horse				neutral
	Crowd		Tries to free D		
	Minister	Refuses to help D			
	President Nixon		Pardons D		

Compiling the Results of the Analysis

The record sheet contains the raw material extracted from the dreams. This raw material must be organized in such a way that it will provide maximum information about the feelings and thoughts of the dreamer. Bear in mind that one seeks to understand himself from his dreams. The purpose is *not* to interpret the dreams as something apart from and independent of the person who has the dreams. Dreams are not visitations from external sources, as was believed at one time; they are the products of a person's mind while he is asleep. They are *his* thoughts and *his* feelings.

Characters

Several hundred characters will appear in one hundred dreams. Some of these characters will make frequent appearances. The first step, then, is to count the number of dreams in which each named or known character appears, and list them in order of frequency.

Here is an example obtained from the analysis of one hundred dreams of a middle-aged woman:

> Husband appeared in 34 dreams
> Daughter appeared in 22 dreams
> Sister appeared in 20 dreams
> Mother appeared in 17 dreams
> Tom (D's supervisor) appeared in 15 dreams
> Brother appeared in 4 dreams
> Father appeared in 2 dreams

The number of times a person appears in one's dreams is an index of the intensity of the dreamer's feelings for that person. It is evident that the woman in the foregoing example is "wrapped up" in her family. The only nonfamily character is Tom, the dreamer's supervisor at work.

One might be curious about the few appearances of the dreamer's father and brother. Her father died when the dreamer was a young child, and she rarely saw her brother after he left home.

Other compilations of characters can be made. It is interesting, for example, to determine the total number of times that male and female characters appear. (These figures include repeated appearances of the same males and females and not just the sum of different males and females.) This tells whether the dreamer is more strongly involved with males or with females. By and large, male dreamers have many more male than female characters in their dreams, whereas female dreamers have about an equal number of both sexes in their dreams.

It is also interesting to compare the number of known persons to strangers. A large number of strangers suggests that the dreamer has few friends or close relationships, and that he feels alienated or "estranged" in his dreams.

A large number of babies and children indicates the dreamer's preoccupation with them. Not unnaturally, women dream more about babies than men do. On the average, about six out of every hundred characters will be animals. If the number runs higher than this, it suggests the dreamer is preoccupied with the animal—that is, the wild or impulsive—side of his nature.

Interactions

The feelings that the dreamer has for people who enter his dreams can be precisely defined by determining the number and kinds of interactions he has with each of them. The woman referred to previously had the following interactions with the five most frequently appearing individuals in her dreams. (The reason that the total number of interactions is greater than the number of dreams is that more than one type of interaction can take place with the same character in the same dreams.)

Husband	22 aggressive,	11 friendly,	1 sex,	3 neutral
Daughter	8 aggressive,	15 friendly,		2 neutral
Sister	10 aggressive,	10 friendly,		2 neutral
Mother	3 aggressive,	16 friendly,		1 neutral
Tom	2 aggressive,	5 friendly,	9 sex,	2 neutral

The reader will observe that there are both aggressive and friendly interactions with all of these persons. This is to be expected, since virtually all significant human relationships are *ambivalent*; that is, both positive, friendly feelings and negative, antagonistic feelings coexist toward the same person.

Observe, however, that there is more aggression than friendliness with her husband, and more sexual and friendly feelings than aggressive ones with Tom. She feels more positive than negative emotions towards her mother and daughter.

One can make this same sort of analysis for classes of characters such as males versus females, known persons versus strangers, individuals versus groups, and animals versus humans. Bear in mind when making these comparisons that the number of interactions with males and females, for example, is determined by the number of males and females who appear in the dreams. If there are twice as many males than females, the number of interactions with males will necessarily tend to be greater.

In order to correct for these differences, one should divide the number of interactions with a given class of characters by the number of characters in that class. For instance, if there are 50 aggressive interactions with males and 15 with females, and there are 100 males and 60 females, the following divisions should be made:

$$\frac{50}{100} = .50 \quad \frac{15}{60} = .25$$

In other words, there is one aggression with every two males, and one aggression with every four females. That is, there are twice as many aggressions with male characters.

It is also interesting to compare the number of dreams in which any aggression occurs, with the number of dreams in which any friendliness occurs. This analysis tells whether the dreamer is more preoccupied with hostile or friendly feelings. Another comparison that can be made is between the number of times that the dreamer initiates the encounter and the number of times that another character begins the interaction. The dreamer may see himself as being more often the victim than the aggressor, or vice versa. This comparison can be done for encounters with individual characters and with classes of characters; for example, males versus females. The dreamer may, for example, initiate more friendly interactions with males, and receive more friendliness from females.

Of interest also is the relative number of physical aggressions (including murder, assault, arrest, imprisonment, stealing, and destructiveness) to the number of verbal aggressions. Does violent aggression prevail? Does the dreamer have more violent aggression with some characters or classes of characters than with others?

The prevalence of sex dreams, the nature of the sexual activities, and one's sexual partners will reveal interesting information about the dreamer's sexual feelings and orientation.

The dreamer may also wish to make a compilation of aggressive, friendly, and sexual interactions which he observes between characters but in which he does not participate. If there are any significant numbers of these witnessed interactions, it suggests that the dreamer prefers to watch others doing what possibly he would like to do himself but is afraid to.

From all of these compilations a number of inferences about the feelings of the dreamer can be made. Here are some questions the dreamer might ask himself after the compilations have been completed.

1. Do the individuals or classes of individuals that I dream about most frequently represent the intensity of my feelings for them?

2. Are there some persons with whom I have frequent contact in waking life who do not appear in my dreams? Why is this?

3. Do any of the strangers in my dreams remind me of people I know?

4. Do I dream about people I have known in the past but whom I have not thought about or seen for some time? Why do these people enter my dreams? Do they have any connection with my present life?

5. Do I dream about people who are actually dead but who are alive in my dreams? How do I behave toward them?

6. Do I dream about babies and children? What roles do they play in my dreams?

7. Do some familiar persons appear in distorted forms? What are the reasons for these distortions?

8. Do some familiar persons appear to be younger or older than they are? Do I sometimes appear to be younger or older than I am? Does this have any significance?

9. Are the celebrities who appear in my dreams those I admire and liken myself to?

10. What roles do supernatural and fictional characters play in my dreams?

11. How do I perceive members of minority groups in my dreams?

12. How do I interact with persons of authority, such as policemen, teachers, army officers, in my dreams?

13. When I dream about a person changing into another person, are the two persons related in some way in my mind?

14. How do I interact with groups or crowds?

15. What roles do animals play in my dreams? Do any of the animals remind me of people I know?

16. What individuals or classes of individuals do I have the most aggression with? The most friendly interactions? About equal amounts of aggression and friendliness? Does this agree with my feelings about them in waking life?

17. Can I divide the dream characters into friends and enemies?

18. Am I more often the victim of attack or the aggressor? Does this vary with individual characters or classes of characters? What do I do in my dreams when someone attacks me? What do they do when I attack them?

19. What causes me to become aggressive in my dreams? What are the reasons other characters become aggressive toward me?

20. Do I initiate more friendliness than I receive? Does this vary with individual characters or classes of characters?

21. With whom do I have the most violent kinds of aggression? Am I more likely to be the victim or the aggressor in these violent aggressions?

22. Are my sex dreams more satisfying or frustrating? Do the sex partners in my dreams correspond to my sex partners in waking life? Do the kinds of sexual activities I practice in my dreams differ from those in waking life?

23. Do my friends and relatives behave in my dreams as they do in waking life? Do I behave toward them as I do in waking life?

24. Do some of the human or animal characters represent aspects of myself?

25. Do the feelings toward people expressed in my dreams represent my feelings toward them in waking life?

26. Do my dream interactions with people reflect my feelings or my actual behavior toward them in waking life?

27. Does the analysis of interactions with people in my dreams help to explain my feelings and behavior toward them in waking life?

28. Are there any consistent changes in the frequency with which certain people or classes of people appear in my dreams with the passage of time? Are there any changes in the type of interactions I have with them? (Such changes are not likely to occur over short periods of time.)

Settings

A dream usually has an identifiable setting. It may be a room in one's home or in another house, a church, a theater, a store, an office, a factory, or a school. It may be an outdoor setting such as a park, a forest, a seashore, a street, or a yard. It may be a city or a foreign country.

The setting of each dream should be listed. If there is more than one setting in a dream, they should be listed in order. If a dream has no setting whatsoever, that should also be indicated.

After the settings have been itemized, they can be classified in various ways. Here are some suggestions:

Outdoors versus indoors
Familiar versus unfamiliar
Past familiar versus present familiar (A past familiar setting is one that the dreamer knew during some previous time in his life—his old home or school or place of work)
Work setting versus home setting
Work setting versus recreational setting
Underground settings, such as caves and tunnels
Water, either in the water or on a boat
Air, as in an airplane

Specific settings which recur frequently can also be noted. These may include one's bedroom, streets, one's place of work, and so forth.

The analysis of settings yields information regarding the preoccupations and interests of the dreamer. If many of the dreams take place in the dreamer's home, this indicates that he is preoccupied with domestic or family affairs. If, on the other hand, there are many dreams of the dreamer's place of work, his interests or feelings center more on his work than his home. Numerous unfamiliar settings suggest the dreamer feels estranged or lost. (Unfamiliar settings are like unfamiliar characters, in this respect.) To dream frequently of places out of the past implies that the dreamer is living in the past. Recreational settings indicate a preoccupation with pleasurable and sensual activities.

The significance of various types of settings can be determined by observing what the dreamer feels and does, and what happens to him in different places. What happens to the dreamer when he is underground, and how does he feel about it? Does he have claustrophobia? Does he come to some harm? Does he feel apprehensive? Is he trying to escape or does he feel safe and secure?

Are his feelings when he is underground different from those when he dreams of being in his own house? Does he have dreams of his house being broken into? Does he flee into his house to escape from some danger? Does he dream of spacious mansions or of run-down houses and shacks?

What happens to him and how does he feel when he is in the water? In an airplane? On a bridge? In a church? In prison? Out in the woods? In an elevator? Climbing stairs? Walking along a street? Driving through the country? On a train? In a store? In a classroom?

Do different things happen to him when he dreams of being in a kitchen, bathroom, bedroom, basement, or attic? Does he feel more apprehensive or threatened when he is out-of-doors than when he is indoors?

These are some of the questions that you should ask yourself about the settings in your dreams. Such an analysis should tell you how you conceive of the world in which you live, just as an analysis of characters tells you how you feel about people.

There is the same ambivalence of feelings with respect to the environment as there is with respect to people. The dreamer is attracted to the out-of-doors because it offers him freedom and adventure, but he also fears it. Wild animals or savages attack him, volcanoes erupt, raging rivers carry him to his death, or he becomes lost in a deep forest. Streets and highways have their own special terrors—robbery, assault, accidents, arrests, falling bridges and buildings—and their own delights—meeting friends, riding through a lovely countryside, unexpected adventures. One's home is a haven but it is not completely secure. Alien and hostile forces in the form of burglars, enemy soldiers, dangerous animals enter it. It has both comforts and discomforts. It is confining, it falls into disrepair, or it catches on fire.

Even places of recreation in which one expects pleasure are not immune from unpleasant experiences. Mishaps and frustrations interrupt one's pleasure. Such dreams suggest that the price of pleasure is punishment.

The dreamer will notice upon analyzing his dream settings that those in which he is underground, in the air, and either on or in the water are often charged with strong emotion. The dreamer will want to pay particular attention to those settings to see whether they depict current conflicts in his life.

Our behavior in dream settings is usually appropriate to the kind of setting we are in, but sometimes it is clearly inappropriate. One dreams of strolling down the street naked or of swimming across a field. In such instances, the dreamer should attempt to discover the reason for the inappropriate behavior. In other cases, a familiar setting will be distorted in some way. These distortions should be examined to see if they have any significance. Dreams with foreign locales should be paid attention to for the same reason.

Because we tend to project our feelings onto the environment, the nature of the dream environment is often a clue to our feelings. Even the climate of a dream can express our emotional state. Sudden changes in the setting of a dream may reflect a change in our feelings. A beautiful house changes into a wretched hovel, day turns into night, dark clouds obliterate the warm sun.

Objects

Many of the objects that are seen in dreams are merely part of the scenery and seem not to play a significant role. The fact that they are even noticed by the dreamer implies, however, that they may have some meaning for him, slight though it may be. For example, if the dream reports contain many references to clothes that people or the dreamer are wearing, this indicates an interest in clothes, and will upon further analysis suggest why the dreamer has this interest.

Other objects are quite clearly significant because they play a decisive role in the action of the dream. The dreamer interacts with them as he does with many of the characters in his dreams. Sometimes an inanimate object will seem to be animated and to have a life of its own. It has a symbolic quality which constitutes its inner or subjective reality for the dreamer. Ancient dream books and their modern counterparts are based upon this inner reality of things, and furnish the reader with their meanings much as a dictionary does. But objects do not have a subjective reality which is independent of the observer. Consequently, one cannot ordinarily assign fixed meanings to dream objects. Each dreamer has to discover for himself the meaning of the objects in his dreams. Moreover, many objects do not have a single fixed meaning throughout an individual's dreams. They have one meaning in one dream and another meaning in another dream. (The same diversity was noted in our discussion of characters.) We may say that an object is a conceptual system that exists in the mind of the dreamer. It is up to the dreamer to discover the conceptual systems for frequently occurring objects in his dreams.

The first step is to list consecutively by dreams all of the objects that are seen or referred to in the dream. If the same object appears several times in the same dream it should be recorded just once. During this step do not attempt to distinguish between significant and insignificant objects. List them all. Although not usually thought of as objects, include in the list all references to parts of the body (hand, face, leg, throat, finger, heart, hair, teeth, etc.), internal or external secretions (tears, urine, perspiration), and such things as warts, pimples, and other growths or blemishes.

After the list is completed, two things may then be done. First, one can make a list of the objects that appear frequently in the dreams. Such a list might look like this one.

Objects	Number of dreams in which the object appears
Automobile	35
Bed	31
Hand	28
Door	22
Coat	21
Money	19
Window	17
Face	15
Telephone	14
Tree	13
Gun	12
Hair	10
Hammer	10

Secondly, similar objects may be grouped together to form a class of objects. A suggested classification is as follows:

Architectural (door, window, fireplace, wall, ceiling, etc.)
Food and drink
Tools
Machinery
Weapons
Recreational equipment
Conveyances (cars, boats, trains, airplanes, etc.)
Plant life
Clothes
Body parts

The frequency with which an object or class of objects appears in one's dreams is an indication of the dreamer's preoccupations. A lot of references to automobiles or to food and drink or to clothing shows that the dreamer is involved with these objects.

In what ways he is involved with them can be determined by noting the kinds of interactions the dreamer has with these objects, the way they are used, and the ways in which they behave in the dreams. An automobile, for instance, can be ridden in or driven, it can go fast or slow, it can break down, have a flat tire, lose a wheel, catch on fire, or leave the road, turn over, go over a cliff, get stuck in the mud, or be in a wreck. The dreamer may lose control of it, he may be unable to start or stop it, or he may fall out of it. It may be stolen or lost. The driver may be stopped or arrested for a traffic violation. He may get caught in a traffic jam. The dreamer may be run over by an automobile. He may be given or acquire a new car. He may engage in a sexual act or have a fight in an automobile. The car may undergo an unusual transformation or be odd in some way. By listing all of the features concerning automobiles, the dreamer will obtain a pretty good idea of the various meanings or symbolic significance that the automobile has for him. A similar type of analysis can be made for other frequently appearing objects.

Bear in mind that any object that appears frequently in one's dreams probably has a rich constellation of meanings for the dreamer. Objects that are familiar and commonplace to us in waking life may be far from commonplace in our dreams.

Earlier we discussed various methods that have been used to decode the symbolic significance of objects. These include Freud's method of free association and Jung's method of amplification. We are convinced, however, that the best method for accurately and comprehensively revealing the often elaborate subjective reality of a given object for a given person is the dream series method of analysis in which one observes the various roles that objects play.

Misfortune

A misfortune is any mishap, adversity, harm, danger, or threat that happens to the dreamer or to another character, over which he has no control and through no negligence of his own. A misfortune is *not* the result of an aggressive act in which there is a definite intent by someone to do harm. It is purely accidental.

Several classes of misfortune can be distinguished. They are: death; injury, illness, or deformity; loss, destruction, or damage to a possession of the dreamer or another character; threat by something in the environment other than a person or animal; falling or danger of falling; and frustration. Frustration includes a number of different elements: encountering an obstacle or barrier, being lost, being late, missing a bus or airplane. These frustrations occur through no fault of the dreamer or another character.

One should go through each dream in a series and note misfortunes that happen to the dreamer and to other characters. Misfortunes to the dreamer may represent self-punishment. Misfortunes to other characters may be regarded as disguised forms of hostility felt by the dreamer against the person to whom the misfortune occurs.

In order to find out what the dreamer may be punishing himself for, he should look at other features of the dream in which a misfortune occurs. It may be, for example, that the misfortune happens to him after he has been aggressive or has engaged in an illicit sexual affair. Falling can represent insecurity, in which case the dreamer may attempt to find what his insecurity is. Injuries, illness, or deformity to the dreamer's body should take into account the specific part of the body that is affected. Sometimes we punish that part of the body which we feel is responsible for causing us to commit an indecent or harmful act.

One should also note the possessions that are lost, damaged, or destroyed to see whether there is any symbolic significance to them. Why, for example, do women dream so often of losing their purses and men dream of defects in their automobiles? It is sometimes revealing to consider one's possessions as representing parts of the body. Thus, a gun that will not fire or a tire that goes flat may represent the dreamer's feelings of impotence, or a lost purse may symbolize the dreamer's fear (or wish) of losing her virginity.

A study of the frustrations that the dreamer experiences will often reveal why he dreams about encountering obstacles. He may find through such an analysis that the obstacles are self-imposed, that he does not really want to reach where he is going. He may feel fear or guilt about what he is doing. The obstacle can represent a warning to himself. There is usually a reason why the dreamer experiences difficulties when he is going on a trip, becomes lost, is unable to make his legs move, or misses an appointment, which analysis will reveal.

Good Fortune

Good fortune is the opposite of misfortune. It is something good that happens to the dreamer or another character which is not the result of his own efforts or of someone else's friendliness. He finds something of value, money, for example, receives a prize, wins a car, and so forth. One can compare the number of good fortunes with the number of misfortunes. The dreamer should not be surprised that there are many more misfortunes than good fortunes. In our experience, good fortune occurs so rarely in dreams there is not much to analyze.

Success and Failure

When the dreamer is trying to achieve something in a dream, he may either succeed or fail. One should make a list of successes and failure, and compare the number of each. This comparison will tell the dreamer whether he is more success-oriented or failure-oriented. He can then compare the kinds of activities which result in failure with those that result in success. This will give him an idea of how he feels about his capacities and incapacities. He may also want to analyze the amount of success and failure he experiences with the amount of success and failure experienced by other characters in his dreams. Does the dreamer succeed or fail in competitive events? Sometimes we fail because we want to fail. The dreamer should examine his failure dreams for this possibility.

Emotions

The principal emotions experienced in dreams are the same as those experienced in waking life: joy and happiness, grief and sorrow, anger and irritation, fear and anxiety, guilt, shames and embarrassment, excitement, and sexual passion. The dreamer should go through his dream series and note each instance where he felt emotional *during the dream.*

Then he should count the number of times each emotion is experienced. The prominent emotions can be listed from the most frequently occurring to the least frequently occurring. This list will show the strength of the various emotions in a person's dream life.

Important information can be obtained by determining what caused the dreamer to feel emotional. Why did he become angry, afraid, happy, or sad? Usually, one will find by this analysis a variety of causes for each emotion rather than a single cause.

Sometimes, the intensity of the emotion is out of proportion to its cause. A minor incident produces a very strong emotional reaction. In such cases, the dreamer should try to discover the reason for his exaggerated reaction. Why should he explode with wrath when someone makes an innocuous remark to him? Why should he feel panic-stricken when he sees a spider? Why should he be overwhelmed by guilt when a police officer stops him for exceeding the speed limit? One may find that the situation has an underlying symbolic significance which explains the excessive anger, fear, or guilt. The innocent remark contains a hidden allusion to the dreamer's shortcomings. The spider stands for something or someone else. Exceeding the speed limits symbolizes more serious criminal thoughts.

In general, however, the quality and intensity of the dream emotion is commensurate to its cause.

It was said by Freud that behind every fear there is a wish. For example, a woman who dreams of being followed by a man with evil intent really wants to be sexually assaulted. The dreamer can determine whether this idea of Freud holds true for his fear dreams.

Inferences and Interpretations

From the foregoing analyses, the dreamer should have acquired a number of insights about his feelings and conceptions concerning himself, his relations with other people, and his environment. In this section, we would like to suggest other interpretations and inferences that can be drawn from dreams. These suggestions are not to be regarded as concrete rules that are applied in a mechanical manner. Such a thing as "concrete rules" do not exist in dream analysis. There are always exceptions, variations, and impertinent cases where the hard and fast "rule" does not apply. The suggestions are merely instrumental guidelines which may, or may not, prove useful in leading one to additional insights about himself. A person who wishes to enhance his self-understanding by studying his dreams is well-advised to consider these guidelines, since they represent the distillation of thoughts of those who have conducted intensive dream studies.

Conflicts

We have already discussed the conflicts that occur between the dreamer and characters, animals, or objects in his dreams. It is also useful to inquire whether some dreams represent conflicts between different facets of the dreamer's own personality. These *internal conflicts,* as we shall call them, may be likened to a civil war, in which the warring factions are citizens of the same country.

One common internal conflict is between the driving forces of impulses or instincts, and the restraining forces of reason and conscience. A typical expression of such a conflict is the dream of being admonished by an authority figure like a teacher or policeman. Upon analysis, the dreamer will often find that the impulse which is being restrained is either sexual or aggressive in nature. Whenever a figure of authority—an official, army officer, teacher, clergyman, coach, supervisor, and, of course, one's parents—appears in a dream, one may consider him to be representative of one's conscience.

Another frequent conflict is between the desire for freedom from the restraints of family life, and the fear of insecurity. A person would like to have more freedom, yet he fears the consequences that such independence might expose him to. This conflict expresses itself in dreams of leaving a secure place (one's home) and encountering dangers and threats of the outside world. Often the dreamer tries to return to the safe place. Sometimes he overcomes the dangers through his own efforts or through the assistance of others. Although this desire to become independent is particularly strong in young people—consequently, their rebellion and defiance of convention—it is not absent from the dreams of older persons. We never lose our fear of the unknown.

Another conflict that manifests itself in dreams is between the masculine and feminine sides of one's nature. The most obvious manifestation of this conflict is when a female dreamer sees herself as a man or as having masculine characteristics, and a male sees himself as a woman or as having feminine characteristics. There is no reason to be alarmed by dreams in which this conflict expresses itself, since it is the basic nature of man to possess both gender orientations in his personality. What may cause trouble is when one aspect of his personality is repressed or denied so an imbalance is created. Here, as elsewhere, dreams tend to rectify or compensate for such imbalances in the dreamer's personality.

Dominance-submission conflicts also appear in dreams. The dreamer will observe in some dreams he plays a dominant role, and in others a submissive role. Both roles may also be assumed within the same dream. The dreamer may take note of the characters and situations to which he submits, and those which he dominates.

The dreamer should look for the presence of other types of internal conflicts in his dreams. A discussion of such conflicts will be found in a book by Hall entitled *The Meaning of Dreams.*

Splitting of characters

Previously we pointed out that the dreamer usually has mixed feelings about the persons who are closest to him. This ambivalence may be expressed by dividing an individual into two individuals, and attributing all of the good feelings to one of the persons and all of the bad feelings to the other person. For example, good father figures and bad father figures, or good mother figures and bad mother figures, may appear in one's dreams. The good or bad representation may assume the identity of an authority, a prominent person, a stranger, or even an animal.

The dreamer may also split himself into various personalities, and identify each personality with a different character. He may, for example, transform himself into a domineering army officer, a submissive pupil, a baby, a wild animal, a gentle affectionate animal, a woman (if he is a man) or a man (if she is a woman), a criminal, a millionaire, a prominent person, a Don Juan, an outstanding athlete, a deformed person, or even a corpse. He may also project himself into objects and become those objects by identification. The dreamer should look for such transformations that express aspects of his own character.

Body symbolism

The dreamer's or another person's body or parts of the body may be symbolically represented in dreams. A favorite form of such representation is scenery—mountains, hills, valleys, gorges, rivers, parks, caves, tunnels, buildings, and parts of buildings. Gentle undulating hills and valleys may symbolize the woman's body. Peaks, crags, and trees may symbolize the man's body. Openings into the earth or subterranean passages may represent organs of a woman. These organs may also be represented architecturally by rooms, hallways, basements, and closets. Similarly, anything that protrudes from the ground—trees, towers, tall buildings, chimneys, poles, mountains—may symbolize male organs.

Physical acts such as being born or giving birth, nursing, excretion, sexual intercourse, or masturbation may also be represented in dreams through symbolism.

One should be prudent when he is searching for symbols in dreams. Doubtless they do exist, just as symbols exist in waking life, but there is no precise method of identifying them. (For a discussion of the methods that have been used for identifying and decoding symbols in dreams, see Chapter 4.) The dreamer should be convinced that the translation of what he perceives to be a symbol into its referent "feels right" to him, and that it portrays his conceptions and feelings accurately. Even when the dreamer feels that a dream symbol has been properly decoded, he should not stop there. He should try to recognize what the symbol reveals about his feelings regarding the object, person, or activity that is symbolized. Plowing a field and entering a cave may both symbolize sexual intercourse, but each of these symbols has its own significance for the dreamer. One cannot be substituted for the other. Plowing a field signifies an active, aggressive penetration (breaking up the ground with a sharp pointed instrument). Entering an opening in the earth is a more passive act, and implies some apprehension about exploring an unknown region.

Projection

A dream is a projection usually in visual form like a motion picture of the dreamer's thoughts and feelings. It does not and cannot represent the thoughts and feelings of anyone else, although we may, in the dream, attribute thoughts and feelings to others. It would be a misconception, however, to assume that this is really the way they feel. The dream is not a counterpart of external reality which enables one to gain knowledge of the external world or of other people.

Dreams unfold the subjective mental states of the dreamer so that one's interpretation of dreams should always refer back to these subjective states. He should constantly ask himself, "What does this series of dreams tell me about myself?" The work of interpretation consists of discovering the primary thoughts and feelings of which the dream is a projection.

In formulating interpretations, one should strive for preciseness. It is not necessary to consult dreams in order to learn that one feels insecure, guilty, anxious, frustrated, erotic, hostile, unhappy, or conflicted. Waking life provides us with abundant evidence of these existing feelings. What dreams do is pinpoint the precise objects, causes, and consequences of our feelings. They tell us exactly what we fear and why, what makes us experience guilt and how we punish ourselves, whom we hate and whom we love, the specific nature of our frustrations and conflicts, and the source in the past from which these feelings evolve. These nocturnal projections of the mind also inform us about the intensity of our feelings, which are important and which are unimportant, which recur numerous times and which occur rarely.

Memories

A series of dreams is an autobiography; the past is continually being recollected in them. Nothing that one has experienced probably ever vanishes completely from the repository in the mind. Sleep seems to be a favorable state for reviving the past, even the very remote past, because during sleep external distractions are reduced to a minimum so that the mind has only itself to contemplate.

This being the case, one can explore the *origins* of his anxieties and frustrations, his ambivalences and conflicts, and other mental states by the analysis of dreams. Many of the dream memories can be traced to childhood experiences. Others are of more recent origin. Some dreams may even be fairly faithful replicas of events that took place during the day preceding the dream. But even memories for recent events may be linked by association with much earlier memories.

Can dreams foretell the future as well as revive the past? Many people believe they can. By keeping a dream record one will be able to see whether some of his dreams were prophetic. This may be an interesting experiment, but it is difficult to see how prophetic dreams can be used to enlarge one's self-understanding.

Dreams are affected by bodily conditions, even by very slight physical changes, so that a disease of which a person is unaware may be represented in dreams. Dreams of suffocation or shortness of breath may be caused by an incipient respiratory disorder, and dreams of falling or incoordination may be an early sign of an epileptic disorder. Such dreams are diagnostic and not prophetic, however.

Archetypal dreams

Some authorities, notably Carl Jung, believe that dreams are not limited to the individual's memories of his own past life but contain memories that have their origin in racial history and evolution. Jung called such memories *archetypal*. One may wish to watch for dreams that are so strange and bizarre as to suggest a source other than one's own past experience. Some of the dream elements that may indicate the presence of archetypal memories are mysterious or supernatural figures, natives, strange animals and monsters, jungles and swamps, underwater or subterranean settings, and legendary cities.

After a person has been analyzing his dreams intensively as the preceding methods require, he should be able to discover things about his dreams that have not been discussed in this book. We certainly hope this will be the case because there is still much to be learned from dreams. For example, it is not known what meaning, if any, the presence of color in dreams has. By examining the experiences of color in your dreams, you may be able to learn its significance for you. Your contributions to a better understanding of dreams would be very welcome.

Synthesis

Analysis, as we have seen, classifies and computes the elements in a dream series. From the frequencies with which these various elements appear, inferences and interpretations are drawn. What we intend to do here is to suggest how this material may be coordinated. This synthesis consists of a description of the dreamer's principal conceptions of himself, of other people, and of the physical environment. The task is similar to arranging the pieces of a jigsaw puzzle, attempting to produce a coherent, organized, and well-balanced picture.

Since we have already alluded to various features that might be included in such a synthesis, we will use this opportunity to present a list that may assist one in making a final formulation of his thoughts and feelings.

It is essential to base this description on information obtained from the dream series analysis and not from extraneous sources. Care should be taken not to exaggerate some characteristics and minimize or ignore others. There should always be a valid reason for making a particular statement, a reason that is based on substantial facts or well supported inferences.

The description should be precise and concrete rather than vague or abstract. One should try to determine the origins of his feelings and conceptions. He should also try to correlate his feelings and behavior in the dreams with his feelings and behavior in waking life, noting discrepancies and similarities and trying to account for these discrepancies.

The list of the dreamer's feelings and conceptions of himself comprise the following items. Not all of the items will be appropriate for a particular dreamer, or he may need to list additional features.

1. Apprehensions, fears, worries, anxieties, dreads, phobias
2. Embarrassment, shame, guilt feelings, humiliations
3. Anger, resentment, antagonism, hatred, rejection
4. Prejudice, intolerances
5. Jealousy, envy, covetousness
6. Grief, sadness, sorrow, affliction, dejection
7. Friendly, helpful, giving, philanthropic
8. Pity, sympathy, compassion
9. Frustrations, confusions, disappointments, perplexities

10. Inadequacies, inferiorities, incapabilities
11. Failures, mistakes
12. Dependence on others
13. Mental and physical capabilities and accomplishments
14. Successes, achievements
15. Restraints, prohibitions, internal controls
16. Impulses: aggression, destructiveness, sex, eating, elimination
17. Temptations, weaknesses
18. Loss of control
19. Ambitions, aspirations
20. Pleasures, delights, zeal
21. Wishes, desires
22. Inner conflicts
23. Conceptions of one's body: disorders, infirmities, deformities, blemishes, imperfections, aging, senility
24. Voyeurism, watching, looking, peeping
25. Exhibitionism, showing off, ostentatious display, egotism, self-satisfaction
26. Sexual orientation: heterosexual, homosexual, bisexual, narcissism
27. Regression, returning to an earlier period of one's life
28. Character traits such as stubbornness, perseverance, honesty, intolerance, cruelty, dominance, timidity, curiosity, vanity, generosity, courageousness, egocentricity, etc.

The second step in making a synthesis of your findings is to decide how you feel about other people. It is understood that these feelings will differ for different persons and classes of people, and that the same person or class can be conceived in different ways for different dreams.

Here is a list that will help you organize the results of this aspect of your dream study. Not all of the items need apply in your case, or you may need to add others.

People (or a specific person or class of persons) are:
1. helpful, sympathetic, understanding, considerate
2. protective, defending
3. trustworthy, loyal, faithful
4. generous, giving
5. strong, resourceful, capable, successful
6. complimentary, praising
7. cooperative, agreeable
8. erotic, sexual, sensual
9. fun-loving, humorous, witty, spirited
10. aggressive, punitive, destructive, cruel, abusive, exploitative, brutal, quarrelsome, obstinate, mean

11. dangerous, threatening, untrustworthy
12. demanding, coercive, authoritative
13. selfish, self-seeking, egotistical
14. frustrating, obstructive, uncooperative
15. weak, timid, submissive
16. inadequate, failures
17. unfortunate, sickly, poor, depraved
18. dirty, messy, unkempt, foul
19. uncontrollable, impulsive

After completing this stage of the synthesis, the dreamer may wish to compare his self-conceptions with his conceptions of others. In doing this, he should pay particular attention to any tendency to project his own feelings or thoughts on other people. Wc are especially prone to see unpleasant characteristics in others that we ourselves possess.

The third step is to sort out one's conceptions of the physical environment. These conceptions may refer to the whole environment or to specific objects in the environment. The same object may be conceived differently in different dreams.

1. Dangerous, threatening
2. Unsafe, perilous
3. Foreboding, evil
4. Dark, ominous, fateful
5. Ugly, dirty, messy, dingy, decaying, deteriorated, disorderly
6. Obstructive, restraining
7. Restrictive, confining, oppressive
8. Crowded, dense
9. Unstable, changeable, agitated
10. Barren, sterile, wasted, void
11. Indifferent, alien
12. Incongruous, bizarre, unnatural, distorted
13. Beneficial, favorable
14. Spacious, vast
15. Beautiful, peaceful, serene, tranquil
16. Fertile, prosperous
17. Colorful, dramatic
18. Climatic conditions: cold, hot, icy, snowy, rainy, overcast, stormy, windy, sunny

It is interesting to consider whether aspects of the environment reflect the dreamer's feelings and moods, an inner subjectivity projected outward rather than an objective reality seen by an unrelated observer.

The accomplishment of this final synthesis does not necessarily conclude the enterprise of trying to understand oneself through dream analysis. A person can and should return again and again to his dream record with new questions and new insights. A long dream series is an inexhaustible source of knowledge; it is like a library which the user can continuously refer to, always finding new material about himself. It is a permanent, personal library that can be subjected to numerous experiments, inquiries, and explorations.

Moreover, if a person continues to record his dreams year after year, he will be able to observe changes in the dreams that signalize changes in his waking feelings and thoughts. There is no better method for keeping tuned into the evolving life of the mind. There are no inaccessible regions of the mind that cannot be made accessible by continuous dream analysis. New vistas present themselves everytime a dream is recalled.

There is no parallel to the kind of self-knowledge a person acquires from the study of his dreams. It is a fascinating, rewarding task worthy of the strongest commitment.

Notes

Chapter 1

p. 9. The "we" refers not only to the two authors but also to many other persons who have been associated with us in the research activities upon which this book is based. They are Alan Bell, Ralph Berger, Charles Bowdlear, Sharon Clark, Roland Cook, Alex Darbes, Max Dertke, Bill Domhoff, George DuPont, John Fletcher, Robert Fortier, Emil Fredericson, Steve Grey, Georgia Griffin, Robert Grotz, Roger Hess, Richard Jones, Donald Kirtley, Ellen Lane, Richard Lind, Samuel Meer, Mary Osterberg, Albert Paolino, Erving Polster, Henry Pope, Claire Rabe, Walter Reis, Harold Shulman, Madorah Smith, Stan Smith, Florence Strong, and Robert Van de Castle.

p. 9. David Schneider very generously made available to us his large collection of ethnic dreams. The Hopi dreams were collected by the late Dorothy Eggan. The Mexican dreams were collected by Professor Nunez, and the Peruvian dreams by Professor de los Rios. Four Argentine students collected dreams for us in their country. The American Negro dreams were provided by Stephen Gornik.

p. 9 The dreams of the Mount Everest climbers were obtained from James Lester, a psychologist member of the expedition.

p. 9. The results of an analysis of the dreams of a child molester have been published in a book entitled *The Personality of a Child Molester: An Analysis of Dreams* by Alan Bell and Calvin Hall.

p. 9. A comparison of the dreams of Freud and Jung was made by Calvin Hall and Bill Domhoff and published in *Psychology Today*.

p. 9. The dreams of Franz Kafka were analyzed by Calvin Hall and Richard Lind and published in *Dreams, Life, and Literature: A Study of Franz Kafka*.

p. 9. The published sources of the dreams of Julian Green, William Dean Howells, Eugene Ionesco, Jack Kerouac, Robert Lowie, and Howard Nemerov, will be found in the list of references.

p. 9. We wish we could acknowledge by name the many people who made available their dream diaries to us, but for obvious reasons they prefer to remain anonymous. Without their contributions, this book could not have been written.

People keep dream diaries for a number of reasons. The Ohio factory worker wagered on horseraces, and he thought the name of a winning horse would appear somewhere in his dreams, often in a disguised form. Since he did not know how the name would appear or in which dream of the night, he made an effort to recall all of his dreams in as much detail as possible. His dream diary, which spans a twenty-year period, contains thousands of dreams. The San Francisco writer kept a record of her dreams because they provided material for her writing. The psychologists who kept dream diaries did so because they were interested in their dreams for professional reasons. Others wrote to us and asked for assistance in analyzing and understanding their dreams. Several of the dream diaries were kept because the dreamer who was undergoing psychotherapy was requested to do so as a part of his treatment.

p 10. For a technical discussion of the content analysis of dreams see the book of that title by Hall and Van de Castle.

p. 11. For a readable discussion of theories of dreaming see the book *Dreams and Dreaming* by Norman MacKenzie.

p. 12. In 1953, it was discovered that the eyes move periodically during sleep. When persons were awakened while their eyes were moving, they were often able to recall a dream. At first, it was believed that the eyes were moving in conjunction with what was occurring in the dream, which led one writer to suggest that this was a method by which a dream could be transcribed while it was being dreamed. No such thing is possible. The same eye movements are used for many different activities. Some of the events in a dream are not visual. Moreover, it has been found that vivid visual dreams can occur while the eyes are not moving. There is also no correlation between the direction of eye movements and the direction a person is looking in a dream. See Berger's articles "The Sleep and Dream Cycle" and "Physiological Characteristics of Sleep"; also Hall's article "Caveat Lector."

p. 13. A report of this investigation has been published in a monograph, *Studies of Dreams Reported in the Laboratory and at Home*.

p. 14. This was established by C. B. Brenneis in a dissertation written at the University of Michigan in 1967. We also found it to be true in an earlier unpublished study.

p 14. One difference between waking perception and dream imagery is that the dream images are often colorless. Investigations of this phenomenon show that a few people dream entirely in color and a few people never experience color in their dreams. The majority of dreamers have colored elements in some of their dreams, or a few dreams are entirely in color. It has been suggested that we always dream in color but the colors fade out of memory by the time we awaken and recall the dream. Other evidence contradicts this suggestion. The question of color in dreams remains a mystery.

p. 15. This evidence was obtained by John Nowlin and associates in a study of the dreams of patients with a history of minor heart attacks.

p. 16. One investigation of dreaming by animals is described by E. J. Murray in his book, *Sleep, Dreams and Arousal*, page 75.

Chapter 2

p. 19. These figures are taken from *The Content Analysis of Dreams* by Hall and Van de Castle.

p. 21. Our discussion of animals in dreams is based largely upon unpublished studies made by R. L. van de Castle.

p 22. This study was published in an article "Strangers in Dreams" by Hall.

p 22. The study of the dreams of a child molester has been published in a book by Bell and Hall, *The Personality of a Child Molester*.

p. 25. This study was reported in an article "An Empirical Investigation of the Castration Complex in Dreams" by Hall and Van de Castle.

p. 27. See the article by Hall, "A Modest Confirmation of Freud's Theory of a Distinction between the Superego of Men and Women."

Chapter 3

p. 36. For an up-to-date discussion of content analysis, see *The Analysis of Communication Content*, edited by G. Gerbner and others.

p. 38. Our method of analyzing dreams is described fully in *The Content Analysis of Dreams* by Hall and Van de Castle.

p. 39. The Study of Franz Kafka's dreams is reported in *Dreams, Life, and Literature* by Hall and Lind.

p. 45. See *"A Ubiquitous Sex Difference in Dreams"* by Hall and Domhoff.

p. 49. A comparison of Freud's and Jung's dreams is discussed in an article "The Dreams of Freud and Jung" by Hall and Domhoff.

p. 56. This study of mental patients was reported in an article

"A Comparison of the Dreams of Four Groups of Hospitalized Mental Patients with Each Other and with a Normal Population" by Hall.

p. 58. Theoretical categories are discussed at greater length in Hall and Van de Castle's *The Content Analysis of Dreams*.

p. 60. The methodology of contingency analysis is discussed by C. E. Osgood in *The Representation Model and Relevant Research Methods*.

p. 60. This dream diary was published in L. H. Horton's *Dissertation on the Dream Problem*.

p. 60. See *Dreams and Symbols* by L. Caligor and R. May and Hall's review of this book.

Chapter 4

p. 63. An interesting account of dream books has been written by H. B. Weiss, *Oneirocritica Americana*. An example of a psychoanalytic dream book is one by E. A. Gutheil, *The Handbook of Dream Analysis*.

p. 64. Metaphorical symbols are discussed in Hall's article "A Cognitive Theory of Dream Symbols."

p. 66. This faucet dream is discussed in Hall's article "Out of a Dream Came the Faucet."

p 68. These observations were reported by M. Boss in an article "The Psychopathology of Dreams in Schizophrenia and Organic Psychosis."

p. 68. The method of free association is discussed by Freud in *The Interpretation of Dreams*.

p 70. The study of strangers in dreams is reported in Hall's article "Strangers in Dreams."

p. 71. The method of amplification is described in C. A. Meier's *Jung and Analytical Psychology*. The example is taken from the same source.

p. 73. The dream series method is discussed at length in Hall's *The Meaning of Dreams*.

p. 74. The use of hypnosis for deciphering symbols is discussed by C. S. Moss in two books, *The Hypnotic Investigation of Dreams* and *Dreams, Images, and Fantasies*. The examples used here are taken from the first book.

p. 77. This study was done by Claire Rabe.

Chapter 5

p. 82. Dorothea's dreams provided the material for an article "An Investigation of Regression in a Long Dream Series" by Madorah Smith and Calvin Hall.

p. 94. This study by Jung is reported in his book *Psychology and Alchemy*.

p. 96. The investigation of fetal memories in dreams is reported in an article "Are Prenatal and Birth Experiences Represented in Dreams?" by Hall.

p. 96.   This observation was made by L. Salk in an article "The Effect of the Normal Heartbeat Sound on the Behavior of the Newly-born Infant."

p. 100.   Probably the first scientific experiments on the effects of stimulation on dreams were performed by a French investigator, Alfred Maury. The results of his studies were published in 1861. A discussion of recent work in this area will be found in *Experimental Studies of Dreaming*, edited by H. A. Witkin and H. B. Lewis; *Studies of Dreaming* by G. V. Ramsey; and *Experimental Modification of Dream Content by Meaningful Verbal Stimuli* by R. J. Berger.

p. 101.   This case is discussed by M. Boss in *The Analysis of Dreams*.

p. 101.   Studies of women's dreams during the menstrual cycle and pregnancy have been done by R. L. Van de Castle and associates.

Chapter 6

p. 105.   See, for example, the article by C. A. Meier and others, "Forgetting of Dreams in the Laboratory."

Chapter 7

p. 136.   Some of the information on the symbolism of bridges was obtained from a paper written by a student, Hattie Rubenstein.

p. 138.   The dream of the carnation was taken from a book *Symbolic Behavior* by T. Thass-Thienemann. This book and another, *The Subconscious Language* by the same author, are rich sources for understanding the psychological significance of words.

p 138.   See Hall's article "Slang and Dream Symbolism."

References

Bell, A. P. and Hall, C. S. *The Personality of a Child Molester: An Analysis of Dreams.* Aldine, Chicago, 1971.

Berger, R. J. "Experimental Modification of Dream Content by Meaningful Verbal Stimuli." *British Journal of Psychiatry,* 1963, Vol. 109, pp. 722-40.

Berger, R. J. "The Sleep and Dream Cycle." In *Sleep: Physiology and Pathology* edited by A. Kales. Lippincott, Philadelphia, 1969.

Berger, R. J. "Physiological Characteristics of Sleep." In *Sleep: Physiology and Pathology* edited by A. Kales. Lippincott, Philadelphia, 1969.

Boss, M. "The Psychopathology of Dreams in Schizophrenia and Organic Psychoses." In *Dreams and Personality Dynamics* edited by M. De Martino. Thomas, New York, 1959.

Boss, M. *The Analysis of Dreams.* Philosophical Library, New York, 1958.

Brenneis, C. B. *Differences in Male and Female Ego Styles in Manifest Dream Content.* Ph. D. Dissertation, University of Michigan, 1967.

Freud, S. *The Interpretation of Dreams.* Vols. IV and V, The Standard Edition of the Works of Sigmund Freud. Hogarth Press, London, 1953.

Gerbner, G. and others. *The Analysis of Communication Content.* Wiley, New York, 1969.

Green, J. *Personal Record.* Harper, New York, 1939.

Gutheil, E. A. *The Handbook of Dream Analysis.* Liveright, New York, 1951.

Hall, C. S. "Diagnosing Personality by the Analysis of Dreams." *Journal of Abnormal and Social Psychology,* 1947, Vol. 42, pp. 68-79.

Hall, C. S. "What People Dream About." *Scientific American,* 1951, Vol. 184, pp. 60-63.

Hall, C. S. *The Meaning of Dreams.* Harper, New York, 1953.

Hall, C. S. "A Cognitive Theory of Dream Symbols." *Journal of General Psychology,* 1953, Vol. 48, pp. 169-186.

Hall, C. S. "A Cognitive Theory of Dreams." *Journal of General Psychology,* 1953, Vol. 49, pp. 273-82.

Hall, C. S. "The Significance of the Dream of Being Attacked." *Journal of Personality,* 1955, Vol. 24, pp. 164-180.

Hall, C. S. "Current Trends in Research on Dreams." In *Progress in Clinical Psychology,* Vol. II, edited by D. Brower and L. Abt. Grune and Stratton, New York, 1956.

Hall, C. S. "Out of a Dream Came the Faucet." *Psychoanalysis and Psychoanalytic Review,* 1962, Vol. 49, pp. 113-116.

Hall, C. S. "Dreams Don't Lie but Dreamers Do." *Old Farmer's Almanac,* 1963.

Hall, C. S. *Dreams of American College Students.* Publication No. 2, Primary Records in Psychology edited by R. Barker and B. Kaplan. University of Kansas Publication, Social Science Studies, 1963.

Hall, C. S. "Strangers in Dreams: An Empirical Confirmation of the Oedipus Complex." *Journal of Personality,* 1963, Vol. 31, pp. 336-45.

Hall, C. S. "Slang and Dream Symbols." *Psychoanalytic Review,* 1964, Vol. 51, pp. 38-48.

Hall, C. S. "A Modest Confirmation of Freud's Theory of a Distinction between the Superego of Men and Women." *Journal of Abnormal and Social Psychology,* 1964, Vol. 69, pp. 440-42.

Hall, C. S. *The Meaning of Dreams.* New edition with a new introduction. McGraw-Hill, New York, 1966.

Hall, C. S. "A Comparison of the Dreams of Four Groups of Hospitalized Mental Patients with Each Other and with a Normal Population." *Journal of Nervous and Mental Disease,* 1966, Vol. 143, pp. 135-39.

Hall, C. S. "Are Prenatal and Birth Experiences Represented in Dreams?" *Psychoanalytic Review,* 1967, Vol. 54, pp. 157-74.

Hall, C. S. "Disquiet After Hours." *Mademoiselle,* January, 1967.

Hall, C. S. "Representation of the Laboratory Setting in Dreams." *Journal of Nervous and Mental Disease,* 1967, Vol. 144, pp. 198-206.

Hall, C. S. "A Life in the Night of John Cook *et al.*" *Nova,* November, 1967.

Hall, C. S. "Experimente zur telepathischen Beeinflussung von Traumen." *Zeitschrift fur Parapsychologie und Grenzgebiete der Psychologie,* 1967, Vol. 10, pp. 18-47.

Hall, C. S. "Caveat Lector!" *Psychoanalytic Review,* 1967, Vol. 54, pp. 655-61.

Hall, C. S. "Dreams and Dreaming." In *International Encyclopedia of the Social Sciences,* 1968.

Hall, C. S. "Special Review of "Dreams and Symbols." *Psychiatry and Social Science Review*, 1968, Vol. 2, pp. 19-22.

Hall, C. S. "Dreams." In *Encyclopedia Americana*, 1969.

Hall, C. S. "Content Analysis of Dreams: Categories, Units, and Norms." In *The Analysis of Communication Content* edited by G. Gerbner and others. Wiley, New York, 1969.

Hall, C. S. "Normative Dream-Content Studies." In *Dream Psychology and the New Biology of Dreaming* edited by M. Kramer. Thomas, New York, 1969.

Hall, C. S. and Domhoff, B. "A Ubiquitous Sex Difference in Dreams." *Journal of Abnormal and Social Psychology*, 1963, Vol. 66, pp. 278-80.

Hall, C. S. and Domhoff, B. "Aggression in Dreams." *International Journal of Social Psychiatry*, 1963, Vol. 9, pp. 259-67.

Hall, C. S. and Domhoff, B. "Friendliness in Dreams." *Journal of Social Psychology*, 1964, Vol. 62, pp. 309-14.

Hall, C. S. and Domhoff, B. "The Dreams of Freud and Jung." *Psychology Today*, June, 1968.

Hall, C. S. and Lind, R. E. *Dreams, Life, and Literature: A Study of Franz Kafka*. University of North Carolina Press, Chapel Hill, N. C., 1970.

Hall, C. S. and Van de Castle, R. L. "An Empirical Investigation of the Castration Complex in Dreams." *Journal of Personality*, 1965, Vol. 33, pp. 20-29.

Hall, C. S. and Van de Castle, R. L. *The Content Analysis of Dreams*. Appleton-Century-Crofts, New York, 1966.

Hall, C. S. and Van de Castle, R. L. "Studies of Dreams Reported in the Laboratory and at Home." *Institute of Dream Research Monograph Series*, No. 1, 1966.

Horton, L. H. *Dissertation on the Dream Problem*. Cartesian Research Society, Philadelphia, 1925.

Howells, W. D. "True I Talk of Dreams." *Harper's Magazine*, 1895, Vol. 40, pp. 836-45.

Ionesco, E. *Fragments of a Journal*. Grove, New York, 1969.

Jung, C. G. *Psychology and Alchemy*. Princeton University Press, Princeton, N. J. 1968.

Kerouac, J. *Book of Dreams*. City Lights Books, San Francisco, 1961.

Lowie, R. H. "Dreams, Idle Dreams." *Current Anthropology*, 1966, Vol. 7, pp. 378-82.

Maury, A. *Le Sommeil et les Reves*. Didier, Paris, 1861.

MacKenzie, N. *Dreams and Dreaming*. Aldus, London, 1966.

Meier, C. A. *Jung and Analytical Psychology*. Andover Newton Theological School, Newton Centre, Massachusetts, 1959.

Meier, C. A., Ruf, H., Ziegler, A., Schellenberg, P., and Hall, C. S. "Forgetting of Dreams in the Laboratory." *Perceptual and Motor Skills*, 1968, Vol. 26, pp. 551-57.

Moss, C. S. *The Hypnotic Investigation of Dreams*. Wiley, New York, 1967.

Moss, C. S. *Dreams, Images, and Fantasy*. University of Illinois Press, Urbana, Illinois, 1970.

Murray, E. J. *Sleep, Dreams and Arousal*. Appleton-Century-Crofts, New York, 1965.

Nemerov, H. *Journal of the Fictive Life*. Rutgers University Press, New Brunswick, N. J., 1965.

Nowlin, J. B. and others. "The Association of Nocturnal Angina Pectoris with Dreaming." *Annals of Internal Medicine*, 1965, Vol. 63, pp. 1040-46.

Osgood, C. E. "The Representation Model and Relevant Research Methods." In *Trends in Content Analysis* edited by I. de Sola Pool. University of Illinois Press, Urbana, Illinois, 1959.

Rabe, C. "A Study of Sexual Attitudes as Revealed by Symbols in Dreams." *Institute of Dream Research Report* No. 2, 1963.

Ramsey, G. V. "Studies of Dreaming." *Psychological Bulletin*, 1953, Vol. 50, pp. 432-55.

Salk, L. "The Effect of the Normal Heartbeat Sound on the Behavior of the Newly-born Infant: Implications for Mental Health." *World Mental Health*, 1960, Vol. 12, pp. 1-8.

Smith, M. E. and Hall, C. S. "An Investigation of Regression in a Long Dream Series." *Journal of Gerentology*, 1964, Vol. 19, pp. 66-71.

Thass-Thienemann, T. *The Subconscious Language*. Washington Square Press, New York, 1967.

Thass-Thienemann, T. *Symbolic Behavior*. Washington Square Press, New York, 1968.

Weiss, H. B. "Oeneirocritica Americana." *Bulletin of the New York Public Library*, 1944.

Witkin, H. A. and Lewis, H. B. *Experimental Studies of Dreaming*. Random House, New York, 1967.

Suggestions for Further Reading

The books marked by an asterisk (*) were written for the general reader. The others are more technical.

Altman, L. L. *The Dream in Psychoanalysis*. International Universities Press, New York, 1969.

Bell, A. P. and Hall, C. S. *The Personality of a Child Molester: An Analysis of Dreams*. Aldine, Chicago, 1971.

*Beradt, C. *The Third Reich of Dreams*. Quadrangle Books, Chicago, 1968.

Bonime, W. *The Clinical Use of Dreams*. Basic Books, New York, 1962.

Boss, M. *The Analysis of Dreams*. Philosophical Library, New York, 1958.

*de Becker, R. *The Understanding of Dreams*. Hawthorn Books, New York, 1968.

*Diamond, E. *The Science of Dreams*. Doubleday, Garden City, N.Y., 1962.

*Faraday, A. *Dream Power*. Coward, McCann and Geoghegan, New York, 1972.

Foulkes, D. *Psychology of Sleep*. Scribner's, New York, 1966.

French, T. M. and Fromm, E. *Dream Interpretation*. Basic Books, New York, 1964.

Freud, S. *The Interpretation of Dreams*. Hogarth Press, London, 1953.

Grinstein, A. *On Sigmund Freud's Dreams*. Wayne State University Press, Detroit, Michigan, 1968.

*Hadfield, J. A. *Dreams and Nightmares*. Penguin, Baltimore, Maryland, 1954.

*Hall, C. S. *The Meaning of Dreams*. McGraw-Hill, New York, 1966.

Hall, C. S. and Lind, R. E. *Dreams, Life, and Literature: A Study of Franz Kafka*. University of North Carolina Press, Chapel Hill, North Carolina, 1970.

Hall, C. S. and Van de Castle, R. L. *The Content Analysis of Dreams*. Appleton-Century-Crofts, New York, 1966.

Hartmann, E. *The Biology of Dreaming*. Thomas, New York, 1967.

*Hill, B. *Gates of Horn and Ivory: An Anthology of Dreams*. Taplinger, New York, 1967.

Jones, R. M. *Ego Synthesis in Dreams*. Schenkman, Cambridge, Massachusetts, 1962.

Jones, R. M. *The New Psychology of Dreaming*. Grune & Stratton, New York, 1970.

Kales, A. (Editor). *Sleep: Physiology and Pathology*. Lippincott, Philadelphia, 1969.

*Kelsey, M. T. *Dreams: The Dark Speech of the Spirit*. Doubleday, Garden City, N. Y., 1968.

Kleitman, N. *Sleep and Wakefulness*. University of Chicago Press, Chicago, 1963.

Kramer, M. (Editor). *Dream Psychology and the New Biology of Dreaming*. Thomas, New York, 1969.

*Luce, G. and Segal, J. *Sleep*. Coward, New York, 1966.

*MacKenzie, N. *Dreams and Dreaming*. Aldus, London, 1966.

Moss, C. S. *The Hypnotic Investigation of Dreams*. Wiley, New York, 1967.

Moss, C. S. *Dreams, Images, and Fantasy*. University of Illinois Press, Urbana, Illinois, 1970.

Murray, E. J. *Sleep, Dreams, and Arousal*. Appleton-Century-Crofts, New York, 1965.

Oswald, I. *Sleeping and Waking*. Elsevier, Amsterdam, 1962.

*Oswald, I. *Sleep*. Penguin, Baltimore, Maryland, 1966.

*Sanford, J. A. *Dreams: God's Forgotten Language*. Lippincott, Philadelphia, 1968.

von Grunebaum, G. E. and Callois, R. (Editors). *The Dream and Human Societies*. University of California Press, Berkeley, 1966.

Witkin, H. A. and Lewis, H. B. (Editors). *Experimental Studies of Dreaming*. Random House, New York, 1967.

Index

absolute constancy, 80-82
actions in dreams, 13, 37, 52, 53
additional information, 161, 162
aggression, 19-22, 24, 25, 27, 28, 32-34, 38, 49-51, 53, 60, 82, 84, 86, 95, 103, 104, 107, 119, 126, 144, 167, 168, 172, 189
alcoholics, 9, 56, 104
ambivalence, 50, 51, 53, 89, 90, 97, 109, 171, 176, 184
amplification, 71, 72, 179
analingus, 28, 29
analysis of own dreams, 156-191
animal-as-father hypothesis, 22
animal dreams, 16
animals, 20-24, 32, 47-49, 60, 86, 87, 90, 95, 165, 166, 171
anxiety dreams, 86
archetypal dreams, 187
Aristotelian dictum, 145
Australian aborigines, 129
automobiles, 39, 92, 94, 129, 133-136, 143, 144, 178, 179

bladder symbolism, 68
body narcissim, 121
body parts, 41, 42
body symbolism, 185
bridges, 136, 137

castration anxiety, 25, 121
categories, 55, 56
characters in dreams, 13, 20, 21, 24, 27, 37, 42, 49, 50, 56, 60, 81, 82, 84, 85, 88-92, 107, 164-172, 179, 183, 184
child-father relationship, 22

child molester, 9, 22-24, 30, 31, 39-41, 45, 57, 91, 92, 104, 153
children's dreams, 19-22, 32, 48, 51, 60, 86, 87, 95
class of characters, 22
coitus, 28, 31, 141
collecting dreams, 158-163
color, presence of, 161, 187
compiling results of analysis, 170-174
conceptual equivalents, 17, 78
conceptual system, 177, 178
conflicts, 183, 184
conscience, 27
conscious suppression, 13
consistencies, 80-102
content analysis, 36-62, 78-80, 86, 105, 106, 163-167, 174-183
contingency analysis, 57, 58, 60-62
continuity hypothesis, 104, 125, 126
continuity principle, 18
courage, 156
covert behavior, 104

daytime thoughts, 146
death wish dream, 27
deaths, 25, 43, 54, 73
denotative symbol, 63-66, 68, 76, 77
describing a dream, 160, 161, 188
developmental regularity, 81, 82
discontinuities, 104
Dorothea, 82, 83, 86, 87, 98-101
dream books, 63, 78, 157
dream correspondents, 20
dream diary, 28-30, 39, 60, 73, 80, 85-87, 125, 154, 158, 159

dream interpreters, 63
dream reports, 13, 19
dream series, 16, 22, 24, 33, 37, 38, 46, 50, 54, 58, 63, 73, 74, 80-102, 158, 164, 165, 181, 186, 188
dreams and waking behavior, 103-127
drinking, 58

eating, 33, 34, 58, 59, 83, 99, 107, 125, 189
elements, 17, 18, 36-38, 57, 58, 60, 63, 71-75, 77, 78, 80, 81, 85, 89, 94, 114, 164, 165, 188
eliminative processes of body, 61
emotions felt during dreams, 13, 54, 164, 181, 182
empirical elements, 58, 59
environmental constancy, 92, 93
essential bodily needs, 32, 33
"eternal ones," 89
experienced dream, 12, 137

failure, 33, 34, 38, 53, 181, 189
father, 22, 23, 27, 36, 37, 42, 44, 45, 47, 57, 69, 70, 91, 92, 109, 122, 124, 133, 136, 142
female dreamers, 22, 45, 49-51, 137, 171
female strangers, 50, 51
fetal environment, 96-98, 105, 110, 131
food, 32-34, 59, 60, 83, 99, 107, 125
format, 159
free association, 22, 68-72, 179
frequencies, 36, 37, 57, 81, 83, 84, 89, 114, 188
Freud, Sigmund, 9, 23, 24, 27, 47, 49, 53, 54, 68, 98, 103, 106-108, 154, 179, 182
Freudian theory, 25, 27, 49, 58, 70, 78
friendliness, 49, 50, 82, 107, 167, 168
friendly act, 32-34
frustration, 25, 180, 188

good fortune, 33, 34, 53, 54, 103, 181

hair, 25, 26
Hamlet, 64, 167
hats, 130
head, 41
holes, 40, 41, 77, 92
homosexual dreams, 30
homosexuality, 9, 108, 123, 153, 189
hostility, 27, 49, 56, 89, 90, 168
house, 39, 40, 92, 129, 131, 132, 143
husband, 42-45, 50, 57, 59, 90, 91
hypnosis, 74, 75

id, 24
inferiority complex, 53
insects, 48, 101
insecurity, 11, 12
interactions, 13, 37, 49-51, 57, 60, 63, 81, 82, 84, 85, 88, 89, 92, 93, 101, 107, 110, 111, 160, 164, 165, 167-169, 171-173, 177, 179
internal conflicts, 183

Jasper, 85-87, 101
Jeffrey, 85-92, 101
Jones, Ernest, 107, 108
Jung, Carl, 9, 23, 24, 47, 49, 54, 71, 94, 103, 106-108, 119, 179, 187

Kafka, Franz, 9, 20, 39, 42, 52, 53, 106, 108-110, 153
Karl, 93, 119-126

Locke, John, 142
long dream series, 80-102, 191

male dreamers, 22, 45, 49-51, 56, 107, 171
male strangers, 22-24, 45, 50, 51, 70
man, 143, 144
Marie, 84-88, 91, 92
Meaning of Dreams, The, 10, 184
memories, 186, 187
menstrual cycle, 101
menstruation, 57

metaphorical symbols, 64-68, 75, 77-79, 128, 133, 137, 138
metaphors, 64-67, 74, 77, 139-144
misfortune, 24-28, 32-34, 53, 54, 82, 86, 157, 179-181
mother, 22, 36, 37, 42, 44, 45, 47, 50, 68-70, 90-92, 99, 110, 124, 129, 133, 142
Mount Everest climbers, 105
murder in dreams, 20, 49, 167, 172

nightmare, 54, 102
nocturnal emissions, 66-68, 119, 121

objects, 13, 39, 40, 56, 85, 92, 93, 101, 128-130, 164, 177-179
Oedipus complex, 49-51, 98, 108
orality, 58, 59, 99
overt behavior, 104

persona, 119
Poseidon, 71, 72
presleep stimulus, 100
projection, 185, 186
prominent persons, 46, 47, 84
prophesying the future, 11
psychoanalysis, 101
psychosexual material, 61
psychotherapy, 11, 86, 101, 102

rape fantasies, 51
Raymond, 86, 87, 101
recalling dreams, 158-163
record sheet, the, 169
referent, 63, 65, 74-76, 78, 79
regression, 83, 189
relative consistency, 81, 82
remembered dream, 12
reported dream, 12, 56, 137
representational symbol, 63
reveries, 159

schizophrenia, 56, 68
schizophrenics, 9
self-aggression, 24
self-punishment, 24, 27, 99, 157
set of dreams, 16, 51, 74, 81, 84, 89, 91, 92
settings, 13, 38, 39, 164, 174-177
sex, 28, 41, 42, 49, 57, 66-68, 77, 79, 84, 116, 120, 126, 133-135, 137, 141, 142, 167, 168, 189
sex dreams, 14, 28-34, 37, 49, 57, 66-68, 73, 74, 76, 84-87, 100, 101, 103, 104, 109, 110, 116, 119, 125, 126, 140, 173
sexual activities, 28-31, 49, 66, 67, 79, 121, 126, 135, 140-142
shadow, 24
Shakespeare, 139, 140
sister, 42, 44, 45, 50, 91, 110
slang, 138-142
success, 33, 34, 53, 181, 189
suicide, 56, 136
superego, 150, 151
symbolism, 17, 18, 28, 105, 128, 129, 132, 135, 137, 180
symbolism in dreams and waking life, 128-144
symbols, 63-67, 71-79, 128, 129, 133, 137-139, 141, 142, 144
synthesis, 188-191

teeth, 25, 26
theoretical categories, 57-60
threatening dreams, 11, 12, 16
Tony, 40, 92, 110-114
transvestites, 9, 39, 116-118, 153
typical dreams, 19, 160

Venus and Adonis, 140
verbal report, 36
virility, 40, 41
voyeuristic, 52, 53, 73, 132, 189

"wet dream," 68
wife, 42, 57, 89, 90, 134
wish-fulfillment dreams, 27, 28, 32, 43, 53

MENTOR and SIGNET Titles of Special Interest

☐ **PSYCHOANALYSIS AND PERSONALITY: A DYNAMIC HISTORY OF NORMAL PERSONALITY by Joseph Nuttin.** A penetrating analysis of modern depth psychology and a dynamic theory on the development of personality. "It is a book which no serious student of psychoanalysis or modern psychology can afford to neglect."—**Commonweal.** Appendix, Bibliography, Name and Subject Index.
(#MY950—$1.25)

☐ **MAN'S SEARCH FOR HIMSELF by Rollo May.** A psychotherapist's commentary on the primary problems of the individual in today's society: anxiety, alienation, emptiness and how he may surmount them. Index.
(#Y4405—$1.25)

☐ **AN ANALYSIS OF HUMAN SEXUAL RESPONSE edited by Ruth and Edward Brecher.** An interpretation and commentary in layman's terms of the monumental **Masters-Johnson** research into human sexual response, with evaluations by the world's foremost authorities on sexology. References, Bibliography. (#Y4054—$1.25)

☐ **THE INDIVIDUAL AND THE CROWD: A STUDY OF IDENTITY IN AMERICA by Hendrik M. Ruitenbeek.** A distinguished European sociologist and psychoanalyst probes the central problem of our time—individual existence in a mass society. Bibliography.
(#MQ849—95¢)